Anne Maguire was born in Enniskillen, County Fermanagh, in 1963 and was educated there at Mount Lourdes Grammar School and later at Queen's University Belfast, where she was president of the Students' Union, 1986–7. In 1988 she joined the *News Letter* as a staff journalist, and moved to the northern office of the *Irish Times* in 1991. She has written for the *Sunday Tribune* and *Fortnight* magazine.

D1322522

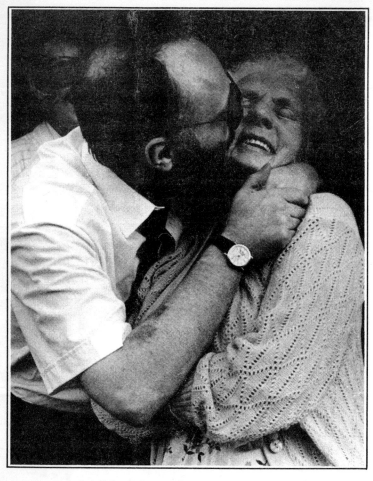

Brian Keenan greets his mother Minnie at her Mayflower Street home
minutes after his arrival in Belfast on 15 September 1990.
(Photograph by John Harrison, courtesy of Pacemaker Press International Limited)

FOR
BRIAN'S
SAKE

The Story of
The Keenan Sisters

ANNE MAGUIRE

THE
BLACKSTAFF PRESS
BELFAST

ACKNOWLEDGEMENTS

Grateful acknowledgement is made to André Deutsch Limited for permission to quote from *Pity the Nation: Lebanon at War* by Robert Fisk; and to Gerald Dawe for permission to reproduce an extract from 'Hostage', first published in pamphlet form, illustrated by Brian Bourke and Mark Byrne, the proceeds of which were given to the Friends of Brian Keenan Fund.

First published in November 1991 by
The Blackstaff Press Limited
3 Galway Park, Dundonald, Belfast BT16 0AN, Northern Ireland
Reprinted November 1991

Typeset by Textflow Services Limited

Printed by The Guernsey Press Company Limited

British Library Cataloguing in Publication Data
Maguire, Anne
For Brian's sake : the story of the Keenan sisters.
I. Title
955.054

ISBN 0-85640-481-0

CONTENTS

DEDICATIONS

To the Friends of Brian Keenan Action Group.

Anne Maguire

To my family for their love and support:
'Time is a great healer.'

Brenda Gillham

To my daughter Ashleigh:
'Brighter tomorrows are better than black yesterdays.'

Elaine Spence

FOREWORD

HELEN BAMBER

DIRECTOR, MEDICAL FOUNDATION
FOR THE CARE OF VICTIMS OF TORTURE

The story of the Keenan family is a remarkable one. As it unfolds we begin to understand that from a very early age Brian was already questioning and exploring the values with which he was presented. He was to emerge into manhood an independent free thinker, concerned about prejudice and injustice, with little fear of speaking his mind. It is ironic that a man with such a profound belief in the rights of his fellow men should lose all liberty. His incarceration for four and a half years, in a manner so frightening, so sinister, is truly beyond our comprehension. Neither can we comprehend the resources that he drew on to withstand the daily agony of that experience.

This book is a moving and sometimes painful record of a family's struggle for survival. Reading it, we realise that at the end of Brian's ordeal his mind and his belief system are still intact. He believes what he always believed: 'I cannot condemn a man because he is different from me . . . that degree to which a man is different from me is that same degree by which I am enlarged and expanded through him.' But no one who saw Brian's face on television shortly after his release can ignore the fact that this is a man who has lived in a vacuum of uncertainty, with death always a possibility.

It is quite natural that loyalties and preoccupations should be with those who have been left behind in captivity rather than with those to whom the captive has returned. Many things important to us in our everyday lives will mean little to someone who has survived the horror of his imprisonment. Division and conflicts within his own society will make less sense than ever to him. It is, I suppose, understandable that there should have been media euphoria and hero worship, with a desire for a happy family ending, but as a society we have shown little comprehension of what that release brought with it. For someone who has lived without human warmth for four and a half years there can be no easy route to what we might call normal human communications and relationships – and he was never a man to pretend. Time and space, always important to Brian, are important as never before. In the end, if we have the capacity to listen, he will teach us much.

Brian's sisters, Brenda and Elaine, are equally remarkable. Were it not for their brother's captivity, they would have continued to lead their lives as ordained – marriage, home, children, with minimal interest in world events. Where did they find the resources to negotiate, to lobby, to learn about Middle Eastern politics, to come to terms with the indifference and, on occasion, the open hostility of members of their own communities, as well as the cynicism of some politicians? How well they weighed up the odds, assessed the people they were dealing with, made strategic decisions that many of us would have vexed and twisted over with less success. Inevitably, their children were affected and the women had to face their feelings of guilt about this. They were sometimes isolated by their battle and were no strangers to fear and uncertainty.

In those four and a half years these two exceptional women developed skills many more privileged people would be happy to possess. The leap they had to make leaves little possibility for a comfortable return to the lives they once knew. In the conversations that I have had with Brenda I have begun to realise the growth of her own development and I would be surprised if she and Elaine did not find a way to put their experience and wisdom at the disposal of those who are suffering similar predicaments. That they both wished to have the love of their brother on his return is as natural as his need to have time and space and freedom.

For the sake of other hostages, we would do well to attempt to appreciate the true nature of the Keenan family's tragedy and the lesson of its survival and the struggle that lies ahead. Each has lived in a state of isolation and profound pain. It is too much to expect that one can take on the pain of the other in the early stages of Brian's release.

It has been a privilege to read this book which gives those of us working with the victims of manmade human tragedies a greater insight into a person's capacity to survive and grow.

LONDON
SEPTEMBER 1991

PREFACE

Towards the end of 1990 I was approached by Brenda Gillham and Elaine Spence about writing 'the story of the Keenan sisters'. I was surprised and delighted to be asked, given that I had only met the women eighteen months earlier and did not know them very well. I collected a binbag-full of press cuttings and a diary (in two folders) from Brenda's home shortly afterwards. The diary, written up by her husband Mick, provided significant insights into a story that was often far removed from the one reported in the newspapers. For most of the four and a half years of Brian Keenan's captivity it is neatly typed, but as events move towards his release on 24 August 1990, it breaks into handwriting.

I began interviewing Brenda and Elaine in March 1991 and continued until the end of June that year. Those sessions were often lengthy and occasionally painful and emotional as the women recalled some of the many difficult times they endured while their brother was held hostage. In May 1991, Blackstaff Press agreed to publish the book and because of the pressure of deadlines, I frequently interviewed the sisters late in the evening and at short notice, and I wish to thank them for giving me their time and courageous openness, without which this book could not have been written. Thanks also to Mick Gillham for access to his diary.

I realised very early on that I would need to speak to many other people in order to write this story. Brian Keenan told me much about his life after his release, and also before he was taken hostage. I am greatly indebted to him for his co-operation and advice. I have to thank him for suggesting that I should be present at a meeting between himself and his sisters in June 1991. It proved to be one of the most valuable exchanges that took place while this book was being written.

For Brian's Sake does not pretend to be the definitive account of the diplomatic manoeuvring that eventually led to Brian Keenan's release. It does, however, contain a considerable amount of material relating to the Department of Foreign Affairs in Dublin. I would like to thank Conor Murphy from its consular section, who worked consistently and energetically on Keenan's case, for his help and support.

I spent many long hours with Frank Wright from the Department of Political Science at Queen's University Belfast. I thank him for his patience and clarity in explaining and unravelling to me the complex situation in the Middle East.

I am grateful to members of the Friends of Brian Keenan Action Group, particularly Frank McCallan, Joe Lenaghan and Jim McIlwaine, who gave me useful and important material, and food for thought.

I would like to thank Church of Ireland Primate of All Ireland, Dr Robin Eames, Brian Lenihan TD, Niall Andrews MEP, David Andrews TD, Aodan Mac Póilin, Terri Hooley, Gerry McLaughlin, Frank Connolly, Joe Austin, Jackie Redpath, John Rowan and Owen Bowcott for their assistance.

A special word of thanks to Gerald Dawe and Dorothea Melvin for their support and friendship, and also to all my colleagues in the northern office of the *Irish Times* in Belfast – Mark Brennock, Gerry Moriarty, Jill, Ingrid and Kieran. I would also like to thank the editor of the *Irish Times*, Conor Brady, and Eugene McEldowney, the paper's chief news editor, for their words of encouragement.

Thanks to my family and all my friends for putting up with me.

Thanks to the Blackstaff Press for its enthusiasm and belief in the book, and to Jonathan Williams for his calmness and painstaking editing skills.

A final and heartfelt thank-you to Helen Bamber for writing the Foreword. She gave of her time freely and has made an important contribution to *For Brian's Sake*.

ANNE MAGUIRE
BELFAST
SEPTEMBER 1991

THANKS TO . . .

The Friends of Brian Keenan Action Group – we are forever grateful.

Dr Robin Eames – for being there when needed and for being a source of light in the darkness of troubled times.

The trade unions – for their support and financial help.

The Royal Mail – for ensuring that mail always reached us under difficult circumstances.

Joe Bradley – for his quiet work throughout the campaign.

Noreen Erskine – for communicating news to us quickly and for all her help and friendship.

Paul Herron – for writing the song 'Remember Brian Keenan'.

Our friends and neighbours – we will always be grateful for their help.

The families of other hostages – for their concern and their support, which helped keep us sane; our thoughts are still with them.

The media – for being patient with us.

Charles Haughey – for his willingness to venture where no one else would.

Gerry Collins – for his care and interest, for his determination in securing a release, and for bringing good tidings.

Conor and Lilian Murphy – for their understanding, and for their commitment to our brother's case.

The pressure group in the Dáil – for its dedication to our campaign.

Bahram Ghassemi, Iranian ambassador to Ireland – words alone can never express the depth of our gratitude, and our thoughts are still with the Iranian hostages.

Anne Maguire – for her willingness to write this book, for her professionalism, for her ability to cope with the pressures involved, for her patience during the bad times, when reliving the past became almost unbearable, and for her sleepless nights.

Everyone, past and present, whose humanitarianism gave us the strength to carry on through four and a half lifetimes, and who are too numerous to mention.

BRENDA GILLHAM AND ELAINE SPENCE

BELFAST

SEPTEMBER 1991

1

STANDING APART

Mid-July in the heart of east Belfast some time in the late 1960s. The bonfire in the playground at Clara Street was in full swing. It was one of the biggest on the Beersbridge Road and was attended by people from all the little streets around. Across Northern Ireland, similar fires were burning to commemorate the anniversary of the battle of the Boyne. A few streets away, Brian Keenan observed the mêlée from a corner of the road. Elaine, his younger sister, was watching him: 'He seemed to be standing there just taking it all in and saying nothing. He stood as an innocent bystander watching it all as it went on.'

Keenan's mind was on other things. For him, the playground had assumed new meaning and a significance over and above its daytime use. 'The children weren't children any more. A kind of ornate ritual was being enacted. There was a kind of intoxication in those flames.' Ten years later, he fought to keep that playground for the children of the area.

Brian and Elaine's parents, Jack and Minnie, moved to Mayflower Street in east Belfast in 1959. Their oldest child, Brenda, was fifteen when they left Evolina Street, four miles away in the Protestant stronghold of Tiger's Bay in the north of the city. Many of their former neighbours followed them. Thirty-two years later, only five houses in Evolina Street are occupied; the rest are either demolished or bricked up. The red, white and blue paving stones are losing their colour, and faded pieces of redundant bunting hang from broken windows. The street sign is chipped and the walls are scorched and scarred. On the main road, Duncairn Gardens, the windows in the remaining inhabited homes are reinforced with metal grilles. On the far side of Duncairn Gardens stands a large piece of green corrugated iron. It separates the Catholic New Lodge from Tiger's Bay.

More than thirty years before, Brian Keenan attended the four-classroomed primary school in the then mixed New Lodge area. It closed down before the extensive population shifts in the city at the beginning of the current Troubles.

There are signs of recent rioting. Broken bottles and stones lie at the bottom of the iron fence. A man looks at the fence and says that the neighbourhood on the other side used to be populated by people of his own religion – Protestants. On the gable wall of Evolina Street, signs exhort the local community to 'Dump Wood Here'. There is no wood, but a little child trails pieces of bedding towards a gap in the street. A proud, elaborate wall mural – the roaring head of a tiger – looks out of place in the dereliction. A peeling sign above a long-closed shop has been replaced by 'UVF' – the loyalist paramilitary Ulster Volunteer Force.

The 'You Are Now Entering Loyalist Tiger's Bay' apes another piece of graffiti in Derry city. Significantly, the people there have added an extra bit of writing to their walls, using some of the words that Brian Keenan spoke shortly after his four and a half years in captivity: 'I cannot condemn a man because he is different from me. Such conceit is self-maiming. That degree to which a man is different from me is that same degree by which I am enlarged and expanded through him.'

Two eight-year-olds stop their play and giggle and laugh when they are asked about Brian Keenan. Older men who live close by say little and talk about how they all came into the neighbourhood only a few years before. A population on the move. Many of Keenan's neighbours, they say, moved to satellite towns like Glengormley and Carrickfergus, but his parents wanted to go back into east Belfast where they had been reared.

Jack Keenan was a post office engineer who was often on twenty-four-hour call. His irregular hours and absences from home made him become an almost fairytale figure in the eyes of the young Brian. Brenda remembers him as a very jocular man, always carrying on and cracking jokes. Elaine recalls that her father was quiet and reserved in the home. Jack Keenan's work often took him into the countryside where he would pick up all sorts of animals like hedgehogs and badgers and bring them back home. Minnie would scream at him to get the animals out of the house, telling him that it was not a zoo.

Minnie had been a shop steward in the linen mills, but she gave up her job there when she got married. The oldest of nine children, she was born and brought up on the Upper Newtownards Road in east Belfast. During World War II, she worked in a munitions factory in the north of England.

Brenda Keenan was born in July 1944. Brian was born six years later in September 1950. Brenda recalls that her brother was always being dressed up like a proper little gentleman, even when they were playing street games. Brian's memory is of other children taunting him about his prominent teeth. As a young child, he played his part collecting wood and tyres for the Twelfth bonfire. Such bonfires are lit all over the North and are an integral part of the traditional celebrations of Protestant victory at the battle of the Boyne in 1690. He took his turn guarding the makings of the bonfire against raiders from nearby streets, sleeping out overnight in a hut constructed from an old wardrobe in the centre of the growing pile.

Brenda attended St Barnabas's Sunday school, run by the Church of Ireland. She remembers Brian crying to come with her. He was not allowed to attend because he was too young. Minnie was furious and a fuming row with the local minister ensued. She ended up taking her older daughter out of the school.

By the time Elaine was born in 1960, Brian was ten and Brenda had left school and was working as a shop assistant in Woolworths. Brian, meanwhile, had failed his 11-plus examination and had moved from Avoniel Primary School to Orangefield Boys' Secondary School. He left there when he was fifteen and worked first as a van boy at Castlereagh laundry and then started his apprenticeship as a heating engineer. One morning, a teacher from Orangefield called to his work to try to persuade him to go back to school. The school had become interested in him because he had won a national poetry competition, open to all children under a certain age in the United Kingdom. An awkward, self-conscious teenager, Brian was filmed by local television reading his poetry. The Keenans first found out about the competition when Brian announced that he was going to be reading his prize-winning poem on the news. His family did not know that he had begun writing poetry several years before because he was fed up with what he was being taught at school.

Brian was persuaded to return to Orangefield, where he sat some state examinations a year ahead of his peers. He later went on to study at the New University of Ulster (NUU) in Coleraine.

The family did not take a great deal of interest in Brian's literary endeavours. Minnie was busy rearing her youngest child, and Brenda had started to spend her weekends dancing in the Plaza Ballroom. She had several boyfriends, and, like most girls in the street, was thinking about getting married. At the age of twenty-two, she married Mick Gillham, an Englishman, originally from Dartford in Kent. They moved into a flat across the street from her parents' home. She gave birth to her first child, Joanne, in 1968.

From his mid-teens, Keenan began to spend less and less time at home, and at weekends often went off with a tent and sleeping bag to the Antrim coast. But his schooling was playing a very important part in his life. Despite the fact that he had never been taught Irish history at Orangefield, he knew that, from a very early age, he had wanted to be part of something different. Many of the teachers at Orangefield were fairly progressive, and Keenan attributes his inquisitive mind wholly to the teaching at his old school. Because of Orangefield's radical and innovative approach, Keenan was encouraged to develop and pursue his interests in Irish literature especially.

At sixteen, he joined the Northern Ireland Youth Campaign for Peace and Nuclear Disarmament, a breakaway group from the Campaign for Nuclear Disarmament. He was also involved in the Belfast Council for Peace in Vietnam. Both groups were very active, but folded up at the beginning of the Troubles. Terri Hooley, owner of the famous Good Vibrations record shop in Belfast, had started both groups and describes Brian Keenan as a dedicated and active member of the two movements. 'We all thought that the revolution was going to happen and that there would be great change.'

Brenda and Elaine knew that their brother was much more interested in the outside world than they were. They also say that he was sometimes arrogant and, when he did not have his head stuck in a book, he was using big words to confuse them. Keenan admits to this, saying that language was one way of breaking away from one's environment. He now feels strongly about what he calls 'linguistic deprivation' and says that, on reflection, he was distancing himself from his family.

Keenan's interest in news and current affairs did cause some rows in the home, particularly with his parents. He always insisted on saying his piece, which was often in direct conflict with what the rest of the family believed. One incident in the mid-1960s stands out. In the run-up to every general election, the Keenans always placed a Northern Ireland Labour Party sticker in their window. Although the British Labour Party did not, and still does not, organise in Northern Ireland, the sticker symbolised Minnie's and Jack's roots in trade unionism. But, politically, the North was increasingly splitting along sectarian lines. The Labour party sticker was replaced with a photograph of the Reverend Ian Paisley.

Paisley was emerging as the voice of extreme loyalism, but Brian Keenan was disgusted because the taking down of the old sticker seemed to him to be a retrograde step. The politics of religion and sectarianism were replacing the politics of labour, and the real issues and needs of working-class people in Northern Ireland were becoming obscured in tribal tradition. For Keenan, it signalled the lack of real choice in Northern politics. 'I did not understand why the family could not think for themselves. It spoke volumes because there was no meaningful outlet for Protestant working-class families who were not sectarian in any way. The annoyance of Paisley going up . . . was my parents' acceptance, suggesting that this was the only choice. What turned them towards this person whom they were allowing to be an articulation of something they did not believe anyway?'

Brenda says that, at this time, a lot of Protestants regarded Paisley as the saviour of their people. The Paisley photograph incident, however minor, signified that Keenan had set himself apart from Protestant politics, ideologies and shibboleths. He says that he was asking his family questions to which they did not have the answers and he believes that this was true of a large number of Protestant working-class people: 'The wool had been pulled over our eyes by a bunch of bowler hats from Stormont for far too long.'

Keenan was much more broadminded than his family, even as a boy. Although the Keenans were never sectarian, they, like a large number of Protestants and Catholics, seldom left their neighbourhoods to mix with people of the other religion. Keenan was already doing this through organisations like the disarmament campaign. He also met a wide spectrum of young people of his own age when he started going to Sammy Houston's jazz club and the old Maritime Hotel in Belfast's city centre, both nightspots for jazz and blues. Keenan believed that jazz and blues were much more experimental and appealing than the showband music of the dancehalls.

When Brian went off to university in Coleraine to study English, it was no surprise to the rest of his family because he had always enjoyed reading and literature. He is not effusive about his university days, saying that he preferred to spend most of his time working alone in the college library. He frequently attended traditional music sessions in the Anchor Bar, a few miles away in the seaside resort of Portstewart, and learnt to play the *bodhrán*.

Brenda, meanwhile, was taking care of her young daughter. She and her husband lived for two years in Mayflower Street and then moved, in 1968, to a multi-storey flat in Tullycarnet in east Belfast. The flat was damp and her young daughter began to suffer from bronchitis. In 1970, like many Protestants, the family moved to the Ballybeen estate on the eastern edge of the city. The estate was removed from those neighbourhoods where sectarian violence was a daily occurrence, and Brenda said that she learnt more about that from television than through any other source.

Elaine was growing up and had joined a loyalist tartan gang when she was a teenager. A widespread phenomenon in the early 1970s, every Protestant community had its own tartan, and this became a symbol of one's background. Elaine belonged to the Woodstock tartan gang, based in the heart of east Belfast. Brian regarded Elaine as a toughie. She left school at the earliest opportunity and went out to work. When she had just turned eighteen, she married Hugh Spence, a labourer from south Belfast. They had been going out together for two years before their marriage. Elaine remembers having to search the town for her brother to tell him when her wedding would be taking place. Elaine and Hugh moved to a terraced house in Lecumpher Street in east Belfast and lived there from 1979 until 1982 when their marriage split up. They had one daughter, Ashleigh. Towards the end of 1982, Elaine started to have a relationship with another Belfast man, Stephen Marshall.

Both women believe that their secondary education prepared

them for little else but marriage and family life. Getting married was expected of young working-class women and they seldom considered doing anything else. 'It was bred into girls when we were young,' Elaine said, 'and it was the natural thing to do; it was a daily routine. You got engaged, waited two years and then got married and waited another while and had children.'

Keenan was moving outside his own environment, mixing freely with both communities in the North. When he left university, he spent a year working in Brussels and in San Sebastian, Spain, where he taught English. He then had a seven-year spell as a community worker for Belfast City Council. This provided him with ample opportunities for crossing the sectarian divide. He worked in tough areas like the loyalist Greater Shankill, Dee Street off the Newtownards Road, and in the nationalist Markets district of south Belfast. His sisters say that he never brought trouble home with him, but Keenan feels that he was a disappointment to his father, who, he says, was not a bitter man: 'He was annoyed about the Troubles like everyone else. Here he had a son, his only son, who seemed to be turning away and moving beyond his values. He was hurt by it.' Elaine remembers feeling envious of her brother because he appeared to have no political or religious ties and could mix easily with Catholics and Protestants alike. In 1983–4, Keenan returned to university, first to NUU where he took an MA in Anglo-Irish literature, and then in 1984–5 to Magee College in Derry, where he was awarded a Diploma in Adult and Continuing Education.

That year, Elaine and Stephen and two-year-old Ashleigh moved into a house in the Ballybeen estate, a few streets away from Brenda. Elaine was unemployed for a long time, but eventually got a job as a childcare worker in the local women's centre on the estate. Unlike Brenda, Elaine was hard-headed and much more aware of what was going on in the world around her, particularly because of her work in the women's centre. Brenda lived for her home and family and was not working when Brian went off to Lebanon because she was rearing her young children, Cheryl and Janeen, who were born in 1979 and 1981. 'I never got involved in any way. My home and my family were the most important things to me.' Brenda was lacking in confidence and spoke out very little: 'I would have thought afterwards, Why didn't I say that? But I never thought that I knew enough. Even when Brian was taken, I still would not have spoken out.'

Jack Keenan died in March 1984, a few months before he was due to take retirement from the post office. In the months before his death, he was concerned that he was not going to have enough money to keep his wife and himself when he retired. One day, he spoke about buying a car and Brenda persuaded him to do it. She and Minnie went with him to buy the car. As he was handing over the cash, he suffered a fatal heart attack. Brenda watched the horror on her father's face and remembers screaming at him, telling him to breathe. He died half an hour later. Elaine says that she suffered for more than two years afterwards because she had actually wanted to see her father's dead body. 'I needed to see him dead, so that I could switch off and accept that he was dead. I was the youngest and I wasn't given a role in the whole funeral.'

Brian moved back to his mother's home in Mayflower Street immediately after his father's death and stayed there on and off

10

for about eighteen months. During this time, he started to apply for teaching posts abroad and made applications for jobs in Lebanon and Libya. When Brenda heard that her brother was thinking of going to Beirut, the only name she associated with the Lebanese capital was that of Tom Sutherland, the dean of agriculture at the American University of Beirut (AUB). She had heard about Sutherland on television. He had been kidnapped on 9 June 1985.

2

'PAINTING HIM GREEN'

Brian Keenan's leaving of Belfast in November 1985 was aptly timed. This was the month when the Anglo-Irish Agreement came into force, outraging loyalist protesters, who then took up camp outside Maryfield, the home of the secretariat, which consists of British and Irish officials who administer the agreement. Brenda phoned her brother to ask him if he needed to take another suitcase with him to Lebanon; he did not. Instead, he told her that he had left food with his mother for his Irish setter, Saoirse. Brother and sister said their goodbyes over the phone.

From Keenan's previous long-stay trips abroad, the family knew not to expect much communication from him. He has the idea that those who write long letters home must be lonely, maintaining that such letters strongly suggest that the senders have not really left home but are still tied to it and therefore less able to experience the new world around them. Any letters and postcards he sent to his family were all posted to his mother's house. He sent a few postcards, the first saying that he had arrived safely. Brenda wrote him a letter to say that everything was fine and telling him that their mother was out of hospital where she had had an operation for the removal of gallstones. Later, she wrote again and facetiously asked her brother if he had a harem. In the New Year, Brian wrote back, asking if his mother was overfeeding Saoirse. In another letter he said that he did not have a harem, but he was working on it.

Keenan's letters threw some light on the strife-torn Lebanese capital. He wrote about the shelling near his west Beirut apartment, and said that many people were carrying guns in the streets. In his letters and his conversations with friends before he left Ireland, he always maintained one thing – there was a war in Belfast and a war in Beirut, but that life had to go on.

When Keenan arrived in Beirut, the Lebanese civil war had been raging for ten years. Between September 1970 and the autumn of 1971, commando units of the Palestinian Liberation Organisation (PLO) were expelled from Jordan. Many fled to Lebanon and the PLO effectively set up its headquarters in Beirut. PLO attacks on Israel, mounted from commando bases in southern Lebanon, intensified. Israeli retaliatory raids in southern Lebanon also increased and Lebanese villagers began to move north, many coming to squat in Beirut. By 1975, the Palestinian population of Lebanon stood at around 350,000. Robert Fisk, in his book *Pity the Nation*, says that the Lebanese were powerless to control the conflict between the PLO and Israel. When the Palestinians attacked Israeli targets abroad, the Israelis invariably assaulted Lebanon.

One of the main detonators of the civil war was the attack by Christian gunmen, believed to be members of the Falangist militia, on a busload of Palestinians at Ayn al-Rummana, in the suburbs of Beirut, on 13 April 1975. All twenty-seven passengers were shot dead. Armed clashes between the Falangists and the PLO, which had become entangled with the Muslims and radicals, erupted everywhere. Fisk describes how, at one point

13

in 1976, PLO gunmen were in open combat in west Beirut, a part of the city they controlled. He says that the Lebanese 'remained locked in their homes while their streets became a battleground for foreigners.' Kidnapping and robbery became an integral part of the war.

That year, the Lebanese president, Suleiman Franjieh, invited the Syrians to intervene in the fighting. In November 1976, Syrian troops entered Lebanon and occupied large parts of the country, but not Christian east Beirut. The troops had a dampening influence on the fighting, but they did not manage to suppress it. In 1978, the Israeli army invaded southern Lebanon and formed a proxy Lebanese militia, the South Lebanon Army. That year, the United Nations Interim Force in Lebanon (UNIFIL), which included several hundred Irish troops, was sent to southern Lebanon. In June 1982, Israel invaded Lebanon the whole way north to the outskirts of Beirut, attacking the Syrian forces in the Bekaa Valley. Their prime target, however, was the PLO. They surrounded west Beirut and demanded the evacuation of PLO guerrillas and Syrians from the capital. In August 1982, about 11,000 PLO troops were evacuated, but women and children remained.

On 14 September, the newly elected Falangist president, Bashir Gemayel, was killed when a car bomb exploded at his headquarters in east Beirut. No group claimed responsibility for his murder. Three days later, Israeli forces allowed the Falangist militia to massacre hundreds of civilians in the Palestinian refugee camps of Sabra and Chatila in west Beirut. Fisk recounts his arrival at the Chatila camp a day after the slaughter: 'There were babies – blackened babies because they had been slaughtered more than 24 hours earlier and their small bodies were already in a state of decomposition – tossed into rubbish heaps alongside discarded US army ration tins, Israeli army medical equipment and empty bottles of whisky.' A multinational force (MNF), consisting of American, French and Italian troops, moved into west Beirut that month as part of an arrangement to secure Israeli withdrawal. The force had no mandate from the United Nations and it supported the Falangist administration.

On 18 April 1983, the pro-Iranian Islamic Jihad bombed the United States embassy in Beirut, killing sixty-three people. Fisk writes about the attack: 'America's political honeymoon in Lebanon had come to a savage and terrifying end. A man, claiming to represent Islamic Jihad, rang a French news agency, saying that the bombing was part of the Iranian revolution's campaign against the imperialist presence throughout the world.' The caller made a particular reference to the MNF. On 23 October that year, 241 American servicemen and 58 French paratroopers were killed in two suicide bomb attacks. It is unlikely that a group like Islamic Jihad could plan and carry out such an assault without assistance. Many informed observers believe it was assisted by Iran or Syria, or perhaps by both. Between 1983 and 1985, the Israelis staged a gradual withdrawal from Lebanon, but continued to occupy the south of the country. In 1983 and 1984, two Lebanese peace conferences, held in Switzerland, failed to produce a resolution of the conflict.

On 8 March 1985, a car bomb killed eighty people in a Shia Muslim district of Beirut. The United States was indirectly blamed for the attack. Between 1977 and 1987, it is estimated that 10 per cent of all Lebanese left their country and a further 20 per cent were forced to move their homes because of the war.

By 1988, more than 100,000 Lebanese had died in the thirteen years of civil war.

Since Lebanon became independent in 1946, the Maronites, who make up two-thirds of the country's Christians, have always held the presidency of the republic. The Christians' major militias, at one time the Falange, and since 1982, the Lebanese forces, are mostly composed of Maronites. The next largest Christian group, Greek Orthodox, is more exclusive socially and less politically committed than the Maronites. Many live in the Muslim area of west Beirut, whereas Christian east Beirut is largely Maronite. The Shias are both the poorest and the largest single religious sect. Before 1984, they had the least share of power in the Christian-dominated government. Their main militia is Amal and its leader, Nabih Berri, has been minister of justice for much of the 1980s. In the wake of the Ayatollah Khomeini's Islamic revolution in Iran, many Lebanese Shias became much more radicalised and thousands joined Hezbollah, or the Party of God.

Hezbollah was formed in 1982 and became the Shias' second militia. Sunni Muslims, the dominant branch of Islam in most of the Arab world, comprise about 20 per cent of the Lebanese population. They have always held the prime ministership and, as such, have had more political power than any other non-Christian group. They are well represented in commerce and the professions. Their militias, however, have been scattered and much reduced since the expulsion of the PLO. The other significant non-Christian grouping are the Druze, originally an offshoot of the Shia branch of Islam, but who consider themselves a completely separate religion. The Druze community is concentrated in mountain areas. Led by Walid

16

Jumblatt, the Druze has one tightly knit militia and party called the Progressive Socialist Party with about 2,500 to 3,000 members. In September 1986, the Druze were fighting with Shias for control of west Beirut. Fisk says that the 'cocktail of armies induced a special kind of weariness'. When the MNF came to Beirut in 1982, for example, there were at least thirty-five foreign armies and local militias in operation.

Despite the civil war, west Beirut was, until the mid-1980s, a cosmopolitan centre frequented by journalists and foreigners on business. There had been waves of hostage-taking and reprisal killings of Lebanese since 1975, but in 1985, the year that Brian Keenan arrived in Beirut, more than fifty foreigners, including twenty-one Finnish soldiers and four Soviet diplomats, were kidnapped in Lebanon. The majority were released, but several were killed. Islamic Jihad claimed its first hostage victim, the head of the Central Intelligence Agency's (CIA) Beirut station, William Buckley, who died under torture in June 1985. The central demand of Islamic Jihad had been the release of seventeen of their comrades, imprisoned in Kuwait for a series of bombings there in December 1983. They have also demanded the release of more than 300 Lebanese Shias being held in Khiam prison in south Lebanon.

The situation became extremely complicated because many hostage-taking groups failed to identify themselves, but it was widely believed that the Iranian-backed Hezbollah was the parent movement for the various Shia Muslim groups who claimed to have carried out abductions. Hezbollah is headed by twelve religious leaders, aided by the former Iranian ambassador to Syria, Ali Akbar Mohtashami. Hezbollah has always had strong links with Iran. Many observers believe that Iran is religiously, ideologically and practically linked to Hezbollah. Titles like 'Soldiers for Justice' and the 'Organisation of the Oppressed on Earth' are thought to be terms of convenience, used to announce threats or demands. It is unlikely that any Western hostages, with the exception of Terry Waite, the Archbishop of Canterbury's special envoy, were kidnapped because of who they were. Rather, they were seized for what they could be exchanged for.

A couple of weeks before Keenan was taken hostage, armed men raided his flat. On his return from work, he found two of his flatmates tied up and discovered that all his money (£800) had been stolen. In a letter to his old schoolfriend, Jim McIlwaine, shortly afterwards, Keenan recounted what had happened and wrote with concern about the lawlessness of Beirut. Yet he always maintains that, during his time as a free man in the Lebanese capital, life was luxurious. When he started working at the AUB, it was very short of English-speaking foreign staff. His workload was heavy and he threw himself particularly into one course which he believed to be very important.

It was a pre-university course and largely attracted young people from villages close to Beirut who did not have enough English to allow them to matriculate into the university. The course was frowned upon by the authorities at the AUB, who regarded the university as the Harvard of the Middle East. For many years, the AUB had been the preserve of the monied classes. Keenan felt very strongly about the course, which was academic yet accessible. The classes, which were mixed sex and mixed religion, attempted to bring the religious traditions of Muslims and Christians together in order to help them articulate to one another their understanding of their own experience and aspirations. This meant devising a course of study that would introduce the students to new concepts and new values, most of which would have been no part of their village life. The intention was to make them tolerant of new ideas and of each other. 'If anyone was going to settle what was going on in Lebanon,' Keenan said, 'it wasn't going to be the Americans or the Israelis. It was going to be Lebanese who were educated.' He gave a class in Russian literature, which no other staff member would take because they associated it with communism.

Keenan's sisters did not know until much later that, shortly before his abduction, Brian had participated in a sit-in at the university, organised by Lebanese students to protest against the kidnap of Leigh Douglas, a political science teacher at the AUB. Douglas had just finished a three-and-a-half-year stint at the university and had signed his second contract a few days before he was captured on 28 March 1986. Keenan was the only teacher to accompany the students on the protest. Other staff hovered on the periphery of the demonstration. Some say that Keenan's presence there may have been a factor in his kidnapping.

Shortly before Keenan was kidnapped, he was intending to move out of his flat into another apartment. The move was delayed because the landlord of the new flat was threatening to put up the rent.

In Belfast, at the beginning of April 1986, Brenda Gillham blacked out in her bedroom, suffering the effects of an illness that had plagued her for almost a year, when one of her lungs had collapsed shortly after her father's death. She was with a friend, who told her later what had happened: 'I was screaming for my Daddy, who had been dead for two years, and when my friend pushed me down on the bed, I told her to leave me alone. I then started shouting about guns, cars and Brian. My father and Brian were always in the same dreams.'

Brian Keenan was kidnapped on Friday, 11 April at about 7 am. He had been in a rush for an 8 am lecture and had left his Irish passport and identity card behind him in the flat. An arrangement, which had been made the night before, whereby a number of foreign lecturers would walk together to the university, did not apply that day because Keenan was going to work earlier than the others. Reports mentioned how a carload of men had been watching his street for some time. He says that he had just come out through the gates of his apartment building when he was bundled into the car: 'A dark green and cream, handpainted Mercedes pulled across the street from where it had been parked. It pulled up beside me. The driver's door opened, blocking my pathway. The driver emerged with a handgun and two men with Kalashnikovs bundled me into the back seat.' Later, in captivity, Keenan was shown a photograph of himself. This discounts suggestions that he was simply abducted because he was the first person to leave his flat that morning or that it was a case of mistaken identity.

When he failed to report for his lecture, some of his students came around to the flat, rightly fearing the worst. Lecturers set about retracing his steps along his route to work. English classes at the university were suspended for the day.

In Belfast, Minnie Keenan was listening to the radio and heard on the mid-morning news that an Irishman had been kidnapped in Beirut. An hour later, Brian's name was released, confirming all her fears. She immediately phoned Brenda. She and Mick drove the four miles to her mother's house in Mayflower Street: 'We were going through red lights and I was telling Mick to go faster. I thought that the journey was never going to end.' Minnie Keenan remained fairly calm on that first day, but Brenda was worried because her mother was saying so little.

Elaine, who had been out shopping when her mother had phoned, only heard the news at 4 pm. 'The news gave his name. My initial reaction was complete confusion and panic and I remember screaming at Stephen that he had been taken. He told me to wait until the next news, that the bulletin was wrong.' Stephen knew that fears for her brother had been playing on Elaine's mind since the kidnapping of Leigh Douglas and Philip Padfield. Padfield, the British director of the Beirut branch of the International Language Centre, had been in Beirut for some thirteen years. 'When you heard it coming over in the news, you were literally gobsmacked. You just fell into a mental daze.'

Elaine told Stephen to take care of Ashleigh while she went to a neighbour's house to phone her mother. Her neighbours tried to calm her down. As she left her home, she told Stephen that she did not know when she would be back. On the way to her mother's, Elaine kept telling herself to be sensible. She was worried about what she would face when she arrived in Mayflower Street: 'The door was open when I arrived and I remember shutting it because it was our problem and we, I suppose, were shutting out the world.'

The atmosphere in the terraced house reminded Elaine of the time just after her father's death: everyone was in a state of shock and the family had no idea who to contact. Their first phone call was to the American consulate in Belfast. Assuming that Keenan was travelling on a British passport, the consulate gave them a number in London. The line was dead. Mick then decided to ring the Foreign Office in London. An unnamed official there told them that Brian was travelling on an Irish passport and therefore was not their responsibility. The family discovered for the first time that Brian had entered Beirut on an Irish passport.

The Foreign Office advised them to phone the Department of Foreign Affairs in Dublin. 'In the beginning we did not know where to turn,' Brenda said. 'When we made those first phone calls and were rejected, it was so hard to take. It was bad enough when we heard that Brian had been kidnapped, but we could not believe it when the British said that he was not theirs. It was very hard to sink in because Brian was just an ordinary man, and suddenly all these governments were becoming involved and he was becoming owned and disowned.'

Friends and relatives arrived at Mayflower Street and sat in Minnie Keenan's small but comfortable front room. The family felt as if they were going through a bereavement, but there was no body. 'It was as if he was dead,' Elaine said. 'The house was full of people, yet it was empty.' They had just put down the phone from their call to London when Sam Mateer, an old schoolfriend of Brian's, arrived. They discovered that Sam, a local artist, had acted as guarantor on Brian's Irish passport, and Dublin had contacted him to formally break the news to the family. Minnie Keenan, still recovering from being in hospital, sent her daughters home to their own families. She wanted to be on her own.

In the Department of Foreign Affairs in Dublin, there was also confusion about the Belfast man. The Irish were well versed in handling kidnappings within their own country. (Six days after Keenan was abducted, Jennifer Guinness, who had married into the wealthy brewing family, was released. She had been kidnapped from her Dublin home by a gang of criminals on 8 April.) Keenan's was only the second kidnapping to take place outside the state. The previous year, Aidan Walsh, the deputy director of the United Nations Relief and Works Agency, had been captured on his way to work in west Beirut. Walsh was released after one day. When officials in Foreign Affairs heard the name Brian Keenan, they assumed that he was a Catholic and suggested to Sam Mateer that a priest should be used to comfort the family. It was also unusual for a Protestant from the North to carry an Irish passport. 'We had to tiptoe around that one,' a Foreign Affairs official confessed. Newspapers speculated about the problems of carrying two passports, but what matters is which passport you use to enter a country. Keenan had left his British passport behind in Belfast, although he had never renounced his citizenship. Today, he is bemused by the passport issue and asks whether a stamp on a certain piece of paper defines a man: 'Such easy definitions are inaccurate, usually boring and on close examination generally meaningless. It's what we are as persons that has meaning.'

That day in Beirut, the first secretary of the Irish embassy, John Rowan, gained access to Keenan's flat and found his Irish passport beside his bed. Rowan came from west Belfast and had met Keenan some time before in Beirut. They had hit it off and became good friends. Rowan, a former boxer, was a man with great physical presence and was not easily intimidated. He went to work immediately to try to establish who had captured Brian. According to Foreign Affairs later, he was getting contradictory signals from the various militia groups he approached. All were pointing the finger at the others. Rowan was gravely concerned, particularly because there had been no claim of responsibility: 'Some people we spoke to did not know and others obviously lied. It was quite clear that we were often being misled.' When Rowan got hold of Keenan's passport, he made copies of several of its pages, including his name, photograph and details of his nationality, and publicised them on Lebanese television and radio and through the newspapers. He gave these same details to militia groups in Beirut.

Back in Belfast, Brenda and Elaine were struggling to come to terms with their new situation. Brenda created all sorts of pictures in her mind to keep sane. She remembered times when Brian had returned unexpectedly from his travels. Because no group had admitted responsibility for the abduction, she tried to tell herself that it was all a big mistake. 'We thought he would just arrive at my mother's door wearing a pair of sunglasses and that he would be dressed like a sheikh.' Elaine was concerned that Brian had been kidnapped because he had said something to upset somebody: 'I thought, What the hell has he done now? He's opened his mouth in the wrong place at the wrong time. Brian loves to get into debates and that's what everyone who knew him automatically thought.'

From the very beginning, both women, but particularly Brenda, had great difficulty sleeping at night. But worse was to come. Four days after Brian's abduction, the United States bombed Libya. The raid, carried out by at least 150 aircraft, hit five targets, including the Bab al-Aziza army compound, which served then as Colonel Gaddafi's command centre and personal headquarters. The British prime minister, Margaret Thatcher, gave her approval for four US airforce bases in Britain to be used by the bomb-carrying planes. The American president, Ronald Reagan, said that he had personally ordered Operation El Dorado Canyon because he 'wanted to try to make the world a smaller place for the terrorists'. Many observers believed that if the bombing had not taken place, Brian Keenan would have been released within a few days.

Two days after the bombing raids, three bodies were found dumped outside Beirut. An anonymous caller, claiming to speak for the Arab Revolutionary Cells, said it had killed the men to avenge the American raids. It is believed that the three men were murdered by a freelance group hired by the Libyans. Later that day, British journalist John McCarthy was ordered to leave the country as quickly as he could. McCarthy, who worked with Worldwide Television News, was on his way to the airport with his Lebanese driver. In Beirut for a one-month assignment, he was taken in an area controlled by the Shia militia.

Officials in Foreign Affairs in Dublin told the sisters that they were 95 per cent certain that Brian Keenan's body was not one of the three. But an entry in Mick Gillham's diary, which he kept throughout the kidnap, indicates that there seemed to be some notion that one of the bodies was Brian's: 'The identification seems too solid. This is our worst moment so far.' Mick took a phone call from Foreign Affairs, who told him that one of the three bodies might be Brian's. Brenda was outside the back of her house when the phone call came and screamed at her husband in desperation, 'No, it's not our Brian.' Mick went to Elaine in the women's centre to tell her about the phone call. Brenda believed that if a death was straightforward, it would not have hurt so much. 'Foreign Affairs left us for forty-eight hours and then they confirmed that it was not Brian. It was like living in limbo.'

In newspapers the next day, there were pictures of Philip Padfield and Leigh Douglas in plastic body bags. The third body had not been identified. Minnie Keenan again wanted to be alone and Brenda remembers being very worried about her. Her daughters tried to keep as much of the horror from her as possible. Brenda sought the comfort of her husband and children. A highly emotional woman, she could not understand why her mother was not reacting more openly: 'The hurt was watching my mother. She never said anything. If you don't cry then it's worse. I remember going upstairs and crying on my own. That was how I got rid of a lot of the tension and emotion.'

In Beirut, John Rowan had brought a colleague of Keenan's from the AUB to identify the bodies. The family was then informed that the third body was that of American Peter Kilburn, an AUB librarian who had been abducted in December 1984.

The Keenans experienced some short-term relief on hearing the news. Brenda and Elaine were in daily communication with Foreign Affairs in Dublin, trying to glean the least piece of information about their brother. For the first year, they would have often phoned Dublin twice a day; it was their only link with Brian's world. In those early days, they did not consider going down to Dublin to agitate for his release. 'It was very hard not to lift the phone, especially when there was nothing coming through.' Foreign Affairs officials in the consular section, who were dealing with the case, seldom returned their phone calls, and said later that, in those early months, they had little of substance to report. They did not understand that what the sisters wished to hear was a voice reassuring them that Brian had not been forgotten about. 'These were people who were diplomats and you expected them to give you information about what was going on. To tell us what . . . they were up against. You always felt that they knew we were so far away and that we could not get down at short notice. We knew that they could divert their phone calls if we were annoying them too much. It was a complete case of helplessness and they did not trust us.'

In the early days, the sisters knew little about the niceties of diplomatic relations and the significance of always referring to Brian as an Irish citizen. The officials in Foreign Affairs seemed very far removed in accent and demeanour from the Protestant working-class women of Ballybeen. Over the telephone, they often seemed not to understand how helpless the women were. Whatever diplomatic to-ing and fro-ing was taking place in the early days was certainly lost on Brenda and Elaine.

Foreign Affairs suggested that Minnie Keenan should write a personal appeal to the Syrians, but they gave her no guidance about what to say: 'We were sitting at the kitchen table writing it. It was very, very hard and emotional for her because she kept tearing it up and throwing it across the table and she was asking, "What are you meant to put in this?"' The letter was sent to Dublin. It was translated and published in Beirut newspapers. In many ways, it symbolised the vulnerability and powerlessness of the three Keenan women.

Yet Minnie Keenan remained strong-willed and talked as if her son was away on holiday. In contrast, her daughters became captives in their own homes. The only way they had of communicating with anyone who had power over Brian's situation was by telephone. 'During the first while, there was always the fear that bad news would come, but we also knew that you could not leave the phone in case you heard good news.' They thrived on media reports about their brother. One, at the beginning of May, said that Brian had been sold from one group to another. This has never been proved. An entry from Mick Gillham's diary at this time shows that the women had accepted Dublin's role in trying to free their brother: 'Our ambassador in Beirut says there is still no news about Brian.' A few days later the diary speaks of concerns by a senior official in Dublin about the role of Terry Waite in Brian's case. A diary entry helps explain this: 'People out there might think that Brian is British. We have painted him as green as we can. This is no offence to anyone, but at the moment it is the best hope.' This was one of the first references to the fact that the Irish government was not keen that the Church of England should be associated with Brian's case. 'It was not an anti-Anglican thing, but we were afraid of Brian being associated with the British,' an official said later.

Every time the sisters received a scrap of information, they passed it on to Foreign Affairs. Once, during the first year, they were told by a woman that Syrian intelligence had held Brian, but that he had been freed by Lebanese villagers. Foreign Affairs assured them that the information did not relate to Brian. Such reports often only added to their confusion and frustration. As far as the women were concerned, they simply believed that help from any quarter was useful. 'You thrived on rumour, even though you knew what it was. It was better than a deathly silence.'

The summer months dragged on. Foreign Affairs officials took their holidays, but there were no breaks for the women. For Brenda, night-time was the worst: 'I feared sleep. For the first

28

two months I never shut my eyes. I was watching cartoons at four in the morning to keep my mind away from the worst. Before that I could have slept on a clothes line.' She would doze, but if an item associated with hostages or the Middle East came on the television, she would jump up. Throughout these trying months, she now realises, she increasingly took her husband for granted. More than five years later, she praises him for his presence and steadiness. A gentle, sensitive man, Mick Gillham would leave the room if he thought that Brenda needed to be on her own. During this time, her weight fell to seven stone and still she was not eating. She felt that no one could understand her feeling of being in limbo and she could not explain to anyone how she felt: 'It just affects people in different ways. I would have cooked food for the world, but I could not have eaten it.' During the first few months, her children – the youngest, Janeen, was only four and a half – had to make readjustments. They grew up extremely quickly. 'They would sense if I was feeling low and they would leave me alone. My kids have always been very loving and they would comfort me with their arms around me, but they also grew up far too fast.'

Elaine was still working in the women's centre, but Brenda had no way of venting her frustrations or thinking about other matters. Yet Elaine, too, found it hard to adjust to her new circumstances: 'When I look back, I was taking far too much on, but I had to keep my brain active. I decided to start getting books on the Lebanon and it was like mission impossible. I would have studied very, very hard into a situation which was only confusing me. You were reading before work, in work and after it.' The books on Lebanon were exhausting her; she was pushing herself into a position that she could not cope with psychologically.

Because Brenda was not working, her home became the focus for most of the phone calls relating to Brian's case. This was also taking its toll: 'I would have exploded at the least little thing. The only thing that was in my mind was that I want my brother home. People would say to me that I looked wretched, but I did not see that myself.'

In July 1986, Syria deployed several hundred commandos into west Beirut, raising hopes that it might lead to the release of the hostages. But a Lebanese official was quoted as saying that the forces had entered without the approval of the Lebanese government. Since Foreign Affairs was only rarely in touch, the sisters decided to become more active and, in September, with a few friends, they formed the Friends of Brian Keenan Action Group. They talked it over with three of Brian's schoolfriends – Jim McIlwaine, Sam Mateer and Mickey Ellison – in Mateer's house in south Belfast. The suggestion for the group came from Bernard Haunch, an old friend of Brian's who taught at the AUB, and who visited the women in Belfast that autumn. As soon as the group had been formed, the sisters felt great relief that others were sharing their burden.

Through the group, they began to learn more about their brother's character. 'These people were sitting there talking about this person whom we did not know,' Elaine said. 'It was like people talking about you and talking over you. You could not join in these conversations. You had a common denominator but you had nothing in common.' When they heard his friends talk about the Brian they knew, they realised that he was a very different person from the brother they had grown up with. They heard stories about him always being the life and soul of a party, whereas he had been very quiet at home. With some relief, they discovered a side of Brian that they had not seen before: that he was an excellent communicator.

At that first meeting, the campaign group decided to contact the three Northern Ireland Members of the European Parliament (MEP), the Reverend Ian Paisley, John Taylor and John Hume. They also spoke to a lot of Brian's other friends and busied themselves by designing a badge, taking great care to ensure that its colours were neutral. When they got replies from the MEPs, they were shocked at their lack of concern. The leader of the nationalist Social Democratic and Labour Party (SDLP), John Hume, was the only one of the three to offer them a glimmer of hope. He told them that he would contact the Syrians through his work in the European Parliament and said that, if he got an invitation to go to Lebanon, he would go. The other responses woke up the sisters to the realities of the narrowness of mind of sectarian politics in Northern Ireland: 'We got an acknowledgement from Paisley, but nothing at all from John Taylor. They just did not want to know about Brian Keenan.' During one election, when John Taylor was canvassing in Ballybeen, Mick Gillham asked him about his brother-in-law's case. Taylor asked why Keenan was holding an Irish passport. 'Taylor had this idea that Brian was a Catholic and he wanted nothing to do with him,' Brenda said. 'Mick put him straight, saying that he was a Protestant from east Belfast, and he told him that this was not the point because Brian was a human being.'

The women, who had been reared not to be sectarian and who had instilled religious tolerance in their own children, were outraged that Brian's passport should be an issue. 'I thought that everyone would be on our side because there was a human being out there who had done nothing wrong. He was an ordinary man and not a politician.' They were determined not to let the passport affect their campaign to free Brian. They started a petition calling for his release and spent their evenings knocking doors and explaining their brother's plight. At one point, Elaine brought the petition around the Connswater shopping centre, in a largely Protestant area of Belfast. One man said that he would not sign it because it was 'too political'. They constantly feared that people would refuse to sign the petition and soon learnt to bite their tongues if people responded negatively or indifferently. They were always thinking of new ways to publicise their brother's plight. 'Your mind was saying: Who can we write to now? You were keeping your mind active, trying at all times to forget about the worst.'

The campaign attracted media attention from early on, and the sisters had to learn how to face the television cameras, no matter how depressed they felt. At first, they found it very difficult. Brenda remembers her first television interview with a BBC reporter, Noreen Erskine, who was to play an important and supportive role in the campaign. 'I could hardly get two words out and I was shaking. Elaine was supposed to do it with me, but she was in bed with a throat infection. It was terrible, but Noreen was very good to me and afterwards she asked how I had managed to do it. It was like talking into an answering machine, but you did it for Brian.'

They got some comfort from knowing that their brother would continue to talk to his captors and that he would always emphasise his Irish identity. Brenda also began reading about the history and culture of the Middle East and admitted that the more she read, the more confused she became. They spent a lot of time trying to work out why Brian had been taken hostage.

To this day, they do not know why he was kidnapped. 'I honestly felt that Brian was taken as British,' said Brenda. The sisters are full of praise for John Rowan, whose swiftness of action in publicising Brian's nationality may have saved his life, particularly after the American bombing of Libya.

Phone calls and letters from people who knew him in Beirut started to arrive in Belfast. 'Speaking to people who knew him out there, they could not understand why he was taken hostage. On the day he was taken, we discovered that his students came to his house to see why he was not at the university.' Making contact with the families and friends of other hostages, like members of the John McCarthy campaign, also was very important because they could share each other's plight. The campaign groups exchanged names and addresses of people whom they believed could be useful. They also shared their experiences of dealing with government officials. The sisters continued to phone Foreign Affairs in Dublin. After the first few months, Mick's diary entries focus on events in Beirut and the Middle East because there was little or no information forthcoming about Brian.

But there were still many lonely times. 'No one understood you. You could be sitting there with the television going and people all around you and you felt that you were not there,' Brenda said. 'It was as if you were looking in, yet you were sitting there.' The sisters gradually became aware of their vulnerability because of their brother's Irish passport. 'We knew that the Irish passport would make everything very difficult because of where we lived. We knew that there would be trouble.' The women found that the silence of some people on the estate was one of the hardest things to come to terms with.

The hate mail started that summer, arriving once or twice a year. Many people told Brenda to tear up these letters, but she always kept a few. 'I wanted to keep them as a reminder of how low people can sink when they try and torture a tortured mind.'

But despite the difficulties they knew they would have to endure, they realised that the Irish passport was Brian's lifeline. 'The British straightaway did not want to know. The Irish were prepared to do something. We had to lift the phone to them to keep us sane. In my situation, it was utter shock to Stephen that I had a brother on an Irish passport.' Elaine often tried to explain the situation to Stephen. In the first year, the two of them would have started their weekly debates about the Irish passport. They never saw eye to eye on the issue. Sometimes serious, sometimes lighthearted, the arguments continued until Brian Keenan's release.

At the beginning of November 1986, an American hostage, Dr David Jacobsen, was released from captivity in Beirut. His freedom is believed to have been largely won because of the intervention of Terry Waite. A day after the release, the 'arms-for-hostages' deal was revealed in the pro-Syrian Lebanese magazine *Ash-Shiraa*, which broke the news of the former US national security adviser Robert McFarlane's secret visit to Teheran two months earlier. The magazine revealed that McFarlane had visited the Iranian capital on board an aircraft which was also carrying arms. Within days, Iran's speaker of parliament, Hashemi Rafsanjani, said that McFarlane had brought a Bible inscribed by Reagan, two Colt pistols and a cake in the shape of a key. Supplies of arms by the United States to Iran were also part of earlier deals which had gained freedom for two Americans, Benjamin Weir and Lawrence Jenco. Weir had been kidnapped on 8 May 1984 and was released on 14 September 1985; Jenco had been kidnapped on 8 January 1985 and was released on 26 June 1986. The revelations overshadowed Jacobsen's homecoming.

The sisters thought that Lambeth Palace could step in and do something for them too. At this stage, they did not trust Dublin and were desperate enough to contact institutions in Britain. In November, Lambeth Palace issued a statement saying that it would do all it could to free Keenan. But a diary entry at this time typified the family's despair: 'All we need is solid proof that he is alive, if only for the sake of his mother.'

The passport issue became very clear when the two sisters discovered that their brother had held out a piece of paper which said 'I am Irish' to Camille Sontag, a French hostage who had been released with Marcel Coudari on 10 November 1986. Eighty-four-year-old Sontag, a retired car dealer, had been kidnapped six months before. Coudari had been kidnapped in February 1986. As the men were freed, France announced that it was going to pay back to Iran $330 million of a billion-dollar loan. The sisters heard on the news that there was a note. All reports at that time stated that the note Keenan showed to Sontag also included the line 'Please tell my family.' Keenan says that this is incorrect. Instead, it read 'My friend is English' and referred to John McCarthy. 'We were so delighted in November 1986,' Elaine said. 'People were phoning up saying, "Listen to him as he comes off the plane", but we could not understand a word he was saying.' She said that she was almost sitting on top of the television, trying to see every detail of the Frenchman's release. She tried to write down phonetically what Sontag was

35

saying and ran around the estate in an attempt to get someone to translate it for her. It was the first time that events had taken a lighter turn since Brian's abduction. 'We were just grateful that someone had got out.' Sontag was their first proof that their brother was alive. He later said that he had seen Keenan's note three weeks before his release.

Officials in Dublin contacted the family very quickly to say that they could not confirm the passing of the note. 'The media were only interested in the "Please tell my family" bit,' said Elaine. 'They thought that they could hit us with it on a soft spot, but they did not. We knew that Brian would not have shown affection in that way.'

The note had an enormous impact on the women and they vowed to prove that it was true. 'We knew then that we were on the right tack. Once Sontag told the world, it was like giving us a concrete brick to hit Foreign Affairs with. Brian was shouting from Beirut that he was Irish.' They also were told that Sontag had been held in a cell for two weeks, from where he communicated with somebody opposite him whom he described as 'jolly'. Sontag had lost his hearing and so the person indicated through sign language that he was Irish, making a capital I with his fingers. According to Sontag, the man looked about fifty – Keenan was then thirty-six – and seemed to have a good relationship with his guard. At one point, Sontag and his fellow inmate were blowing kisses to each other. Sontag also said that the other man's hair was rusty-coloured, as Keenan's was.

The sisters learnt not to release too much information to the media. When they heard a detailed report about Sontag's experiences, they gave only a limited version to reporters, on the advice of Foreign Affairs. This was primarily to ensure the safety of Keenan and the other hostages. Sontag's release provided the only bit of good news in almost seven months and the first flicker that their brother was alive. Up to the end of 1986, the lack of information was causing the women considerable distress and this led to rows with their partners. 'We were trying to grasp every thread coming from Foreign Affairs. All we wanted them to do was to keep in contact with us. We told them that we needed to know what they were doing for Brian.'

In mid-December, John Rowan, who had just returned from the Middle East, met the sisters in a Belfast hotel. He told them that a reliable source had assured him that their brother was alive. It later transpired that Rowan had received his information from Sheikh Muhammad Hussein Fadlallah, one of the spiritual leaders of Hezbollah. He had told Rowan that Hezbollah was not holding Keenan. On several occasions, Fadlallah distanced himself from the hostage-takers. Rowan expressed some concern about the whereabouts of Keenan's British passport, but the sisters assured him that it was in a drawer in Mayflower Street. They left the meeting with the impression that Rowan knew more than he was prepared to say. He also advised them to keep any media statement about the meeting as short as possible. This was also a frustrating time for John Rowan. He now admits that he was drawing a blank with most of the militia groups he was meeting. The only consolation he could offer the sisters was that he did not think that Brian Keenan had been killed by his captors.

At the end of the year, the Irish embassy moved out of Beirut and established itself in the Iraqian capital Baghdad. This was earth-shattering news for the sisters. The embassy, which had opened in 1974, was one of the last remaining in west Beirut.

Foreign Affairs admit that the Lebanese were 'very put out' at the Irish exit from Beirut. But John Rowan, who is currently consul general in San Francisco, says that the Lebanese capital was in chaos in the months before they moved out: 'There was no way that we could carry on our normal embassy work. It was impossible to move around freely.' Communication by telephone and by telex had broken down and the embassy's only link to the UNIFIL troops in southern Lebanon was by radio. Rowan often had to visit the troops by helicopter because road links were unreliable. According to one official, the decision to close the embassy was taken at the highest level. It is unlikely that Brian Keenan's captivity played any part in the decision to move. The sisters head the news through an early morning phone call from an official at Foreign Affairs. 'This was bound to hinder the chances for Brian. The lifeline that we had through John Rowan was getting very thin. We thought we were going to come to the end of our tether. Here we were sitting with nobody in Beirut.' In view of the Iran–Iraq war, Elaine could not see the sense in pulling someone out of Beirut and putting them into Baghdad. The sisters were told that the embassy was closed down for purely security reasons. A long period elapsed between the closure and the appointment of an honorary consul in Beirut.

The sisters' memories of their dealings with Foreign Affairs officials during the first year are ones of frustration and anger. They phoned Dublin every day, begging them to stay in touch. They are still convinced that if Brian had been from the Republic, he would have been given more attention: 'Brian was the first Irish person who was kidnapped in those circumstances and I suppose it was difficult for Foreign Affairs. They were always good when they had to deal with all the kidnaps inside Ireland.' Things did not improve at Christmas. Brenda remembers: 'We were sitting around the table and Janeen said, "I wonder what Uncle Brian is eating." Cheryl said that he was probably having bread and water.' She said that Christmas was always a difficult time for her because her children asked Santa every year to bring their uncle home. 'You just tried to be as normal as possible and you put on a face and tried to make it special for them.'

Brenda's three children became increasingly aware of their mother's stress. If they noticed her crying, they would leave the room and let her weep in peace. Elaine regrets that her young daughter knew more about the situation than she should have done. There was a drawing competition at her school and Ashleigh painted her Uncle Brian. 'She remembered Brian standing outside my mother's house and he's got his cap on and he's taking them into the shop for an ice cream. She wrote a note saying "Send Brian home because Keenan misses him."' Later, Ashleigh wrote that she loved her mother because she was working hard to free her Uncle Brian. The New Year was a particularly harrowing time for the two women. Brenda said that she could never welcome the New Year with any enthusiasm as long as her brother was being held hostage. Instead, she went off to her room and sat alone, sometimes speaking quiet words to him.

At the beginning of January 1987, Brenda and Elaine arranged to meet the Archbishop of Canterbury Dr Robert Runcie's envoy, Terry Waite, in Belfast where he was scheduled to give a talk at the YMCA. He cancelled his visit a few days before, but went ahead with another trip to the Middle East, against the advice of the Foreign Office. Because of a lack of information from

Dublin, the women were turning increasingly to Lambeth Palace for assistance. They saw Waite as someone who could be of great help to their case and were hoping to meet him on his return from Lebanon.

On 20 January 1987, Waite himself was kidnapped and so the sisters' second lifeline was severed. On the day he was captured, Waite was being escorted by his Druze bodyguards for a meeting with Islamic Jihad. The bodyguards left him, as agreed, but eventually it was realised that this was only a trick to kidnap him. 'We depended a lot on him,' Brenda said. 'Although we did not have many conversations with him, we knew that he was another resource. We thrived on all the times he went into Beirut. It was like the final bit of rope being cut when we heard the news that he had been taken.' The sisters got in touch with Waite's family. According to Mick Gillham's diary, everything seemed to go on hold when Waite was taken. His abduction had attracted a considerable amount of media attention. There was even speculation that he had been kidnapped because he was a spy. Walid Jumblatt, the Druze leader, had promised to help ensure Waite's safety and had travelled to London to assure his family and Dr Runcie of this.

In January, the sisters decided to go to Paris to see Camille Sontag, the only person who had provided a glimmer of hope about their brother since his kidnap. They also hoped to meet Dr Joelle Kauffmann, wife of the French hostage Jean-Paul Kauffmann, and other interested parties. The campaign group organised social functions to raise money for the trip. Their first fundraiser was in the Markets Community Centre, in the heart of a small Catholic enclave in south Belfast. It was the first time that the women had visited this neighbourhood: 'We never believed that we would be sitting in the Markets. It was hard to take it in as you walked through the door, but the people made you feel at ease.' Their partners, who stayed at home, were concerned for their safety in a part of the city that once had been out of bounds, but their fears were unfounded.

Relations with Foreign Affairs in Dublin continued to be frayed. Towards the end of February 1987, Brenda phoned staff in the consular section to complain that they had not heard from them for more than a month. Officials apologised to them, but confessed that they had nothing of substance to report. According to Brenda, Dublin was never very keen on their Paris trip, and the women say that they went ahead against the wishes of Foreign Affairs. Officials in Dublin claim that this is not true. Several days before they left Belfast, Dublin rang to say that Dr Kauffmann did not want to see them. At first she had intended to meet them at the airport. The women were dumbfounded and so asked Jill Morrell, from the John McCarthy campaign group, to act as a translator for them. It transpired that Dr Kauffmann had gone to the Irish embassy in Paris and had told officials that she could not meet the sisters because she would be on call when their flight came in. She asked someone from the embassy to meet them instead. This did not happen. 'It was as well that we were not depending on Foreign Affairs at that stage because they got it wrong,' Elaine said. 'I suppose they knew that we would come back from Paris two harder women.'

Before they left for Paris, the women met senior Foreign Affairs staff in Dublin for the first time. They said that the officials asked a lot of questions about their family background. The women felt inferior and lacking in confidence in their conversation with the well-briefed Foreign Affairs representatives. 'We knew that they were only picking our brains to see exactly what was going on and what our background was. We knew that we were being sussed out,' Elaine said. They asked about Brian's activities and his life before he had left Belfast. 'They talked about the North and about what Brian's character was like. They didn't really ask where Brian stood on the whole thing. They asked us for our views on the Troubles in the North and what schools we went to. It was like a general chat about living through the Troubles,' Brenda said. The sisters felt far from comfortable with the officials, who often used big words which the sisters could not understand.

When they arrived at Charles de Gaulle airport, nobody was there to meet them. Unable to speak French, they soon got lost. Eventually, they managed to buy a map and decided to go straight to the Arc de Triomphe because they knew that the Irish embassy was close by. From there they made their way to the Avenue Foch. 'A Frenchman met us at the door,' Elaine said. 'By that stage, our blood was boiling because we could not explain to him who we wanted to see.' They say that a diplomat in the embassy told them that he could not understand why they were there. He was told that the women wanted to find out more details about Sontag's debriefing. In Paris, they also met officials from the French Foreign Office, journalists, and Philippe Rochot, a Frenchman who had been a hostage in Beirut for 105 days in 1986. Rochot, whose kidnap was claimed by the Revolutionary Justice Organisation, was the first hostage the sisters had met. He told them that, in captivity, he was allowed to read modern romances, including those by Catherine Cookson. He was trying to remember the name of one of the novels he had read. 'We were firing names at him,' Elaine said, 'and it was so touching and moving when he told us that he would have to go back into his cell to remember the name of the book.' They left him alone for some time and he suddenly remembered the name of one of the books, saying it was called *Harlequin*.

There was no chance to meet Sontag because the former hostage was in the south of France and the women had neither the time nor the money to visit him. Before the trip, they had sent Sontag photographs of Brian to see if he could recognise him. He was unable to do so because all he had seen of the hostage when he held out the note was the bridge of a nose and eyes through a slit in a door.

When the sisters went to the Quai d'Orsay, the headquarters of French Foreign Affairs, they were told that the hostage that Sontag had spoken about kept his captors entertained with his wisecracks. When the sisters heard this, they knew it must have been Brian. 'Jill Morrell was sitting there thinking that it was John and we thought that it was Brian. It was very hard. When they told us that they thought it was Brian, it was good for us, but we felt for Jill.' There was an indication that a taller man was being held with Brian and the sisters also heard something about red hair. According to the French officials, Brian sang constantly and this annoyed the guards. A Beirut-based French journalist told them that Brian had been sold to a Libyan-backed group and that Gaddafi could help to secure his release. The journalist also told them that their brother was being visited by a doctor once a month. This proved to be untrue. He also told them that Brian was alive only because of his nationality, which, he said, was well known in the Lebanese capital.

The Paris trip was a significant milestone for the women: it was the first time that they had obtained information independently of the Department of Foreign Affairs. On their way home, they made a list of almost twenty demands to present to the department. At Dublin airport, not only were their partners waiting for them, but Foreign Affairs had sent someone to greet them. The women were furious about how they had been treated by the Irish embassy in Paris and angrily presented the departmental official with their list. 'We had it all written down about what we wanted and who we wanted to see,' Elaine said. 'They took down everything, but what they did with it I don't know. It was the first time that we told them exactly what we wanted.' Uppermost in their minds was a meeting with the Taoiseach, Charles Haughey. They were told that this would take some time to organise.

A fortnight later, they were back in Dublin to visit the Irish parliament, the Dáil. They met a Labour TD, Michael D. Higgins, who asked them if he could do anything to help them. Higgins remembers that the sisters were depressed when he met them. 'They were having a very bad day. They were very tired and at that time the intricacies of diplomacy and language didn't mean much to them,' he said. He made a request for them to see Haughey and, a short time later, Brenda and Elaine were sitting in the Taoiseach's office. 'You thought surely to God this man of power will be able to do something,' Elaine said. 'At least he had the decency to see us. We told him what we knew and about France and he said that he started to take an interest in the case before Christmas. He did not ask to see us again, but he left the way open. We gave him our side and we did not expect anything back.' This meeting with Haughey, which was not made public, gave the women a great boost.

As the first year of Brian's captivity drew to a close, his sisters found that they were being recognised increasingly in public places, mostly because of their numerous television interviews. Strangers would often come up to them and say that they knew Brian when he had been a community worker and how he had helped them out in some way or another. But whatever enthusiasm their case was receiving from the general public in the North, it was not shared by their elected representatives, including their MP, James Kilfedder. 'There was nothing in the North that we could do. The only person who saw us was John Hume. It was a rude awakening about what life was like in the North.'

3

CONTACTS AND COMPLEXITIES

One day in the middle of June 1987, Elaine Spence left the women's centre, telling her colleagues that she would be back in an hour. She boarded a bus into Belfast and headed for the courts in Chichester Street where she was to get her divorce from Hugh Spence. They had been separated for more than five years. 'The divorce took a long time about coming. It was something which should have mentally affected me but it did not at all. I just threw it over my shoulder. I had no idea what was ahead of me when I got onto that bus. I just took it into town, got divorced and got it back out again. It was the first time that I realised that I was not taking myself into consideration.'

For some time before her court appearance, social workers, who were dealing with the case, were coming to her home and Elaine was afraid that they would recognise her as Brian Keenan's sister. 'I was concerned that they would see who I was and that ... they would say that Ashleigh would be affected.' She was worried that social workers might think that she was neglecting her five-year-old daughter because she was often away from home campaigning for her brother's release. This never happened, but the thought of it caused her considerable anxiety. 'I would think a lot about my divorce now after Brian's release and I would have changed things. I wanted to drop the name Spence and call myself Keenan again, but I thought that it would cause too much confusion and I did not do it.'

Elaine was also very aware of protecting Ashleigh from the glare of publicity: 'I did not want Ashleigh to be in the papers because I did not want her father to know how she was coping with life.' She has one major misgiving about her relationship with Stephen after the divorce. 'I remember Stephen asking me to marry him, but I said no because I had too much on my plate, and that was a big regret.' Elaine found that the little time she was spending with Stephen was far from perfect. 'When we managed to get time on our own, we were being tortured by reporters. Our lives were totally engaged. You would have needed a separate line for private and personal conversations.'

A few weeks earlier, the second year of their efforts to free Brian had got off to a very unpromising start. An entry in Mick Gillham's diary from that time states hopefully: 'An end to a busy year. Let's hope that all the hard work will now bring home some good news in the next year.' The campaign group marked the first anniversary of Brian's captivity by holding a press conference in his old school, Orangefield, in east Belfast. There, they were presented with a cheque for £40, an amount raised by the pupils. Brenda and Elaine were taken along a school corridor to see photographs of their brother in the Orangefield rugby team. Aged sixteen, he was the only player sporting a beard. Later that day, they faced rows of reporters and cameras in a hall in the school. One journalist asked them what they pictured themselves doing in a year's time. Elaine replied defiantly that she did not expect to be sitting answering questions at a press conference. The campaign group had decided to use the press conference to criticise what they saw as Dublin's inactivity. They knew that officials in Foreign Affairs would not be happy with their remarks, but this did not deter them. 'We were learning to have confidence and we were determined to let Foreign Affairs see that we were not going to take all this lying down,' said Brenda. 'We realised that we had to speak what was in our hearts and we had to let them know publicly.' That day, they had been very hurt because no one from Dublin had spoken to them, but this was the first time that they had hit out so strongly against the Irish government.

On the day of the first anniversary, the ambassador at the Irish embassy in Baghdad, Patrick McCabe, flew into Beirut to seek information about Keenan's whereabouts. He stayed there for several weeks, but drew a blank. Because no group had claimed responsibility for the abduction, it was difficult for McCabe to channel his energies in one particular direction. After the closure of the embassy in Beirut in late 1986, the family was given an assurance that diplomats would travel regularly to the Lebanese capital to try to communicate with possible hostage-taking groups.

The sisters were becoming increasingly angry at the lack of contact with Dublin. At the beginning of May 1987, relations took a turn for the worse with the publication of a report in the *Belfast Telegraph* quoting a spokesman from the press office in Foreign Affairs as saying that Keenan's abduction was still a mystery and that they had no trace of him. The sisters rang senior officials, demanding to know why they had not been told before the publication of the story. They were informed that they would get a full report of any news about their brother. 'That was when the pressures really started in the family,' Brenda said. 'We were fighting with each other and saying that we were not being told the whole truth and my mother was saying the same. Foreign Affairs were saying that they had nothing. I remember thinking that we had every entitlement to know what they were doing.'

The family clung to every jot of information it received. Shortly after the anniversary, the sisters saw an article in the *Belfast Telegraph* about a man called Robert McGuckin, who had written to the Iranian leader, Ayatollah Khomeini, calling for Keenan's release. They phoned the newspaper and got McGuckin's address in west Belfast and went to see him. 'He welcomed us in and he said that he wanted to help on humanitarian grounds,' Elaine said. Their desperation for new information was so strong that they started relying on McGuckin, a complete stranger, for help. Later in May, he said that the Iranian embassy in London had phoned to say that Keenan should never have been taken, that it was a mistake. According to McGuckin, the Iranians were also impressed with the way the campaign group was handling the media: 'We do not accuse any group or government in our statements. It is important that we keep it that way and that no statements are made on our behalf by the Americans. The Iranians will be watching our every move,' says Mick Gillham's diary. They became increasingly aware of the politics and culture of Lebanon, and started to take note of dates like the beginning and end of the Muslim thirty-day holy period, Ramadan, when they thought that there might be some movement because it was a time of prayer. The sisters also grew more conscious of how they should conduct themselves when they were being interviewed by the media. It took them more than a year to discover that there was an Iranian embassy in Dublin. It was McGuckin who told them.

Early that summer, Brenda met two senior loyalist figures in the Ballybeen estate when she was collecting signatures for the petition. The men assured her that the campaign group would have no bother collecting names for the petition because it had nothing to do with the Troubles. 'They said not to worry about who you have to meet. And ignore any remarks made by anyone,' a diary entry reads. The conversation gave Brenda some consolation: 'It was a relief because I was going to people's doors. We were always conscious of the surroundings and certainly our family was conscious of it and we had to take all that into consideration.' At the beginning of June, Jim McIlwaine and Brenda went to visit the lord mayor of Belfast, Dixie Gilmore, who said he would like it if all the people in the North cared about Brian Keenan. He signed the petition and told them that he thought that it should be extended beyond Northern Ireland. He also agreed to open a fun run for them, which took place in the middle of July in Ormeau Park in south Belfast.

The women considered going to Teheran to make their own personal plea for their brother and had even priced flights to the Iranian capital. They felt that Dublin was washing its hands of their case: 'We knew at that time that we could not rely on their diplomacy and that we had to take a different path ourselves.' They had dropped hints to officials about going out to Teheran, but this was generally greeted with apprehension and concern. That summer, the Irish Minister for Foreign Affairs, Brian Lenihan, met the Lebanese defence minister, Hasan Usayran, and a few days later, had talks with the deputy foreign minister of Iran at the United Nations. Little came of the meetings, but the women were informed that both men were interested in their brother's case and could not understand why he had been kidnapped. The meetings were significant because they marked the Irish government's widening of the circle of inquiry. For most of the first year, officials had concentrated their efforts in Beirut; even diplomatic approaches by the Irish to Iranian legations yielded little. When the Irish chargé d'affaires in Teheran, Noel O'Byrne, tried to make approaches to Iran's Ministry of Foreign Affairs, he received a very cold reception.

Shortly after 12 July, the Keenans were contacted by Shane Paul O'Doherty, a former member of the Irish Republican Army (IRA) and born-again Christian, through a third party. O'Doherty, who was serving a life sentence in the Maze prison for his part in a series of bomb attacks in London in 1973, said that he wanted to meet and help them. But a note of caution was introduced into Mick's diary: 'If any of the family are seen, someone would make a big thing of it. Although we will take any help we can get, this should be thought about very carefully.' The sisters let the matter drop until O'Doherty got in touch again. On 29 July, they met Seán MacBride, a Nobel Peace Prize winner. 'I didn't even know who he was,' Brenda admitted. 'A lot of people talked about the great man that he was. He was very old and he kept drifting off and he said that he would do anything that he could. Unfortunately, he died before he could do anything to help.' They received more approaches from O'Doherty, telling them that he knew Arabic through prisoners he had met while in jail. They decided not to get involved with him because it might cause them harm from others.

At the end of July, they received Brian's registration of Irish citizenship; this event is marked in Mick's diary as being highly confidential. The document is released only in exceptional circumstances. It was sent along with Keenan's educational qualifications and a 9,000-signature petition to the Iranian parliament, addressed to the parliament's speaker, Hashemi Rafsanjani.

On 10 August, Gordon Thomas wrote in the *Irish Independent* that a group of Iranian priests was going to meet to decide whether or not they would put the foreign hostages on trial for their lives. In the absence of any firm news from Foreign Affairs, such stories caused the sisters great anxiety. They phoned Foreign Affairs and asked them to verify the report. They were extremely worried because Thomas had mentioned Brian's name; the story claimed that he was a spy working for the CIA. Afterwards, they reacted angrily to Thomas's article. Jim McIlwaine phoned him, telling him that his report was highly irresponsible.

In September, Robert McGuckin told them that Brian might have been one of four hostages moved up for release, but any calls from Foreign Affairs were simply to say that they still had no news about him. They were spending more and more time away from home, attending meetings in Belfast and Dublin. The sisters found out very early on that the best way to confront officials in Foreign Affairs was not by telephone but face to face. Many people could not understand why they had to go to meetings. 'Everybody thought that you would only have to do it once or twice,' Elaine said. 'You learnt very quickly that you would have to depend on a lot of people to get the children to school, for example. Even the men's jobs were being threatened with all the running about.' From the outset, they decided to play Foreign Affairs at its own game and started bringing notebooks into meetings, taking care to write down what little they were being told. But the lack of news was still distressing to the women and their families. 'There was a lot of emotion building up among the family,' Brenda said, 'and we had no chance to express it because of the pressures. You were coming to terms with living with it. You were not expecting news the following day or the following week.'

Another newspaper report, giving details of an American spy satellite which allegedly had pictures of Brian that showed him to be mentally and physically ill, was published towards the end of 1987. Such reports caused the women great anguish, especially because they were not receiving information from any other source. 'It came at a really bad time of the year for us and we were so worried that he was ill. It was terrifying.' In November, they encountered more trouble. Shane Paul O'Doherty had a letter published in a Lebanese newspaper, *An-Nahar*, calling for Brian Keenan's release. 'When the English papers got it, it was "IRA Bomber Pleads For Brian Keenan". The fact that he was a born-again Christian and that he had changed his ways was not important to them,' Brenda said.

Concerned for their safety, they made numerous phone calls to British newspapers, asking them to play down the story. 'I remember when we did it thinking that there was going to be trouble here,' Brenda said. 'There were people who did not like it and they were people who remembered what he did. We knew that the media would portray it as something that it was not. There should be give and take with the media because they knew the whole political thing here.' The women did not fear retaliation from people living in the Ballybeen estate. 'It's not the people who you are living with or working with, but the ones outside that. It didn't have to take a group of them because even one could do damage. It was portraying Brian as even more nationalist than we did and the more that happened, the more we were in danger,' Elaine said.

In December, the sisters travelled to London to attend a special party for the families of hostages and for disabled children, including some from Belfast and Beirut. It was organised by Professor Paul Cook, president of the British Science and Technology Trust. An eye specialist, Professor Cook started a scheme to use modern technology to help ease the plight of children in Lebanon. The first part of the event was held at the Houses of Parliament at Westminster and, later, Brenda and Elaine met the Duchess of Kent. She asked them if they were helpers at the party.

The next day, the youngsters and Brenda and Elaine went to Lambeth Palace and were all taken on a tour of the building, despite the fact that many of them were blind. Something strange happened in the middle of the tour when they were in the church. A candle was lit for Terry Waite, but as they started to leave, it went out. Everyone scurried around for matches and an Anglican nun produced a box from down the side of her boot. When they were praying for peace, a Lebanese woman told the gathering that her country also needed prayers, but none were dedicated to Lebanon. Elaine remembers becoming extremely annoyed that when the woman asked a second time for prayers to be said, again nothing happened; she wished that they could have stopped in the corridor and prayed there. At the end of the visit, they were all presented with a medallion, but no one explained its significance. They were disappointed that Dr Runcie did not make an appearance. 'He should have shown his face if only for his own,' Elaine said. She was also very angry at the end of the trip because she thought that the children had been ignored.

The next day, the sisters were supposed to attend other events, but they decided to go instead to the Iranian embassy in London. Accompanied by Mickey Ellison, they set off for the embassy. They decided that it would be better to take a man along because it might mean that they would receive better treatment. When they arrived, they mentioned a name from the embassy and were allowed in. 'There were no phone calls beforehand and no plans made. They had every right to close the door on us. We were in such a temper coming from Lambeth Palace because of the way that the children had been treated,' Elaine said. They met a secretary to the ambassador. 'You were always dubious about talking to foreign people because they would tell you what you wanted to hear,' Brenda said.

The sisters had succeeded in meeting the Iranians without the help of the Irish government. The visit was also very important, because the women, for the first time, became aware of the plight of the three Iranian hostages and their Lebanese Shia driver, who carried an Iranian passport, who had been kidnapped by Christian Lebanese forces in northern Lebanon in July 1982. The Iranians consistently linked the issue of the Western hostages with the case of the three Iranians.

The sisters pledged their support to the families of the hostages, whom eventually they would meet. Copies of the *Teheran Times* were strewn on tables in the embassy's reception area and they discovered that the paper carried articles on the hostages nearly every day. They were also informed that their petition had arrived in Teheran. 'It gave us a great deal of hope because we were talking to the Iranians. We knew that most of the groups in Beirut were Iranian-backed and hoped that they would use their influence. It encouraged us to go into any Iranian embassy.' The sisters were told that the Iranians had no quarrels with the Irish. 'When we came out, we were delighted that we got to where we did because we didn't even expect to get in the door,' Elaine said. But the women also believed that Syria was particularly important at that stage because they had been told by a friend of Brian's that its army was moving closer and closer to where the hostages were being kept. 'They had the men on the ground in Lebanon at the time. They were getting closer and closer to the militia men's bases.'

But any elation the sisters felt about being at the Iranian embassy was soon dissipated after Sinn Féin's visit to Beirut. At the beginning of December 1987, Sinn Féin president Gerry Adams sent a telexed statement to a news agency in Beirut, calling for Brian Keenan's release. A few weeks later, two Sinn Féin members, Joe Austin and Denis Donaldson, met representatives of a number of revolutionary groups in Beirut. Some commentators have speculated that the visit was an attempt to stave off the bad publicity the organisation had received because of the Enniskillen bombing on 8 November which had killed eleven people. Austin stresses that the visit was made independently of the family and explains why Sinn Féin became involved: 'Brian Keenan had been a fairly active community worker in the Shankill and the Markets and he had an association with people doing similar work in the west of the city.' He said that the indications they received was that Keenan was alive, but that his captors believed that he was a spy, for two reasons – because he worked for the AUB and because he had two passports. He said that, in late 1986, it had been established through Palestinian groups that Keenan was alive and that he was most likely being held by Hezbollah.

With the help of a Belgian journalist, Austin and Donaldson

put together a team of people who would meet them and help them in Beirut. Shortly before they left, however, a Dublin-based journalist told them that a Lebanese businessman had said that there were indications that Keenan was dead. When the Sinn Féin members contacted Beirut, they got a contradictory view. They also claim that, while on a stopover in Geneva, they received an update from Foreign Affairs to the effect that Keenan was dead. Austin claims that this information was fed to them because Foreign Affairs would have been acutely aware of the political implications if Sinn Féin had helped in Keenan's release. An official in Foreign Affairs strenuously denies that it ever was in touch with Sinn Féin: 'There was no question of us getting into direct or indirect contact with them.'

The journey to Beirut was suffused with complications, but when the two men arrived, they were met by a Swiss woman, who acted as guide. They were taken to the Muslim part of the city where they discovered that one of their helpers was Mahmood Berri, a nephew of the Amal leader, Nabih Berri. They met leaders from Druze and from Amal. Both groups denied that they were holding Keenan. The most important meeting was with Fadlallah, the Hezbollah leader, in his headquarters in an old Christian fort. Austin says that Fadlallah had only a vague and general understanding about Ireland: 'We told him that Brian Keenan was a friend but not a fighter and that he was anti-imperialist. We said that his departure from Ireland was a loss, but that his death would be a tragedy.' The Hezbollah leader told them that his men did not have Keenan and that, in any case, they would not have taken him. After an hour-long meeting, Fadlallah told them that he would pursue the case. Austin believes that the most important thing they managed to do was to convey that Keenan was not a spy. Keenan thinks that shortly after this visit, his beatings stopped. When the two Sinn Féin members left Beirut, they were told to stay on the Continent for eight days. Donaldson did while Austin returned to Ireland. Austin says that they did not inform the press about their visit, but that it was leaked while they were still in Beirut. He wishes that the visit had never been publicised: 'From our point of view, it would have been better holding tight and trying to get him out again at another stage. The leak damaged our ability to have Brian Keenan released sooner.' He claims that the visit by Sinn Féin spurred Foreign Affairs into action.

The sisters learnt about the Sinn Féin visit when Noreen Erskine rang them one teatime to ask for a comment. Later, they went on television and said that they did not want to get mixed up with any organisation. The family reacted angrily to the visit and quickly prepared a short press statement. Elaine said: 'The family never believed that they were out there only for Brian Keenan. They may have been out in that general direction on other business.' Brenda said that the period terrified her: 'It frightened me, it really did. I knew these organisations existed and I was not involved in anything. When I heard, I was shaking in my shoes because two nights before a fella on the estate had been shot at the back of Elaine's. I really panicked. I was afraid of retaliation.' She also felt very angry: 'I never asked these people to do this. I don't get mixed up in my own organisations and I don't want to be mixed up in anyone else's.'

Most of the sisters' worries were about their children and, at one point, Brenda asked Mick to pack up and take them away with him for a while. She, however, was determined to stay in the home. Elaine believes that the Sinn Féin visit may have damaged the campaign. They say that they always preferred their friends to mention any controversial events to them afterwards, to clear the air. 'If people stay silent, that's when it's dangerous,' Elaine said. 'They did then.' The women now admit that it did cause problems in the homes, but their minds were often unreceptive to their men's points of view. 'I know that Stephen wanted to pack up and leave and I said to him, "Where do we go? Do we go to another Protestant estate where the same would happen again?" You were being put into a situation where you were not welcome on any side. Who would have taken us? I would definitely have gone if someone had come and threatened me.' They also had to suffer taunts from people who talked about their 'Fenian brother'. 'We did not want to meet Sinn Féin because of who they are and we have nothing in common with them. If we had done it, we would have had to live with the consequences of it for the rest of our lives. It would have been a publicity stunt all over again,' Elaine said. 'It was certainly a time when you thought that you were in danger. It would have been nice if they said that they did it because they were human beings.'

Lieutenant Colonel William Higgins, the American commander of the United Nations Truce Supervisory Organisation, was kidnapped in southern Lebanon on 17 February 1988. The women made no attempt to contact his family. There was a certain fear of getting embroiled with Americans. Elaine said: 'The fear was more for Brian than for ourselves. Even Americans involved at that time in hostage discussions, such as Terry Anderson's, did not touch the Higgins case. There was always a big question mark over Higgins's head'.

Slowly, however, the women were being taken into the confidence of Foreign Affairs. Before the visit by Vincent Brady, Minister of State at the Department of Defence, to the UNIFIL troops on St Patrick's Day, the sisters were told that it was going to take place. After Keenan's kidnap, such trips took on increasing significance. Vincent Brady met Nabih Berri, leader of the Amal group that controlled much of southern Lebanon. Berri told Brady that he had no news of Keenan, but that he did not have much hope that he was still alive. It was the worst news the Dublin officials received. They intended to tell the sisters, gently, that Brady had got next to no information in Lebanon. They thought that the news should be broken to the women through another member of the campaign group. Brenda saw a report about the visit in a newspaper before the group member had a chance to tell them. She was devastated, but refused to believe that Brian was dead: 'As I read it, I just broke down and cried. The tears were not tears of sorrow but ones of anger. I remember looking up at Brian's photo and saying that Berri was only one man and that he was not telling me that Brian was dead. I got very upset that day. I thought that Dublin should have phoned us. You had to hang on to things like the feeling deep down that he was alive. It got to the stage when you thought, Take me instead, and that was stupid. That's how desperate it became.'

All this time, their mother coped in silence. Brenda admits that she could not have handled the situation so stoically if it had been one of her own children. They were also told about the efforts Ireland's diplomatic staff in the Middle East were making on Keenan's behalf. Patrick McCabe, the ambassador in Baghdad, told them about all the militia groups he had spoken to and the steps he had taken to trace Keenan. He said that, so far, they all had come to nothing, but he reassured them that he would not give up. The sisters praise him for staying in touch. Brenda said, 'Every time he came home, he would give us a full verbal report of everything he had done.'

The hijack of the Kuwaiti airliner Boeing 747 three hours after it took off from Bangkok en route to Kuwait at the beginning of April 1988 was a very worrying time for the Keenan family. It also caused a stalemate in what appeared to be fairly advanced negotiations for the release of the French hostages. The hijackers, Islamic Jihad, said that they were seeking the release of seventeen Shia Muslim prisoners being held in Kuwait. The plane landed at Larnaca in Cyprus. The hijackers threatened to kill the hostages in Beirut if the Special Air Service (SAS) stormed the plane. When they made their threat, they issued photographs of the French hostages Kauffmann and Carton. This made front-page news in many newspapers on the morning of the second anniversary of Brian Keenan's kidnap. Brenda and Elaine never turned off their television sets that day, watching every development during the hijacking, while their mother listened constantly to the radio. At one point, the Algerian government was asked by the ruler of Kuwait, Sheikh Jaber Ahmed Al-Sabah, to act as a go-between. 'Algeria did not want to be the middle man and we knew at the end of the day a third party was needed to solve it,' Elaine said. 'We were literally praying that someone would come in and let the plane run and start talking because it had sat so long on the tarmac.'

During this time there was little the campaign could do for Brian. They also appealed for the plane not to be stormed because of the risk that many people would die. 'The appeal was for everybody on the plane – not just the Western hostages. We sat up all night long waiting for the next news bulletin.' Because the hijacking happened at the time of the second anniversary, the sisters found an increase in public support, as people became aware of their campaign: 'Everybody was realising the dangers of the hostages, how their lives were held just on a piece of string,' Elaine said.

A note written in Mick's diary typified their despair: 'With the pressure of the hijacking and the outcome and the fear of what could happen to the hostages, it has brought a very sad end to a hard year of work. And we know less than we did last year.' The entry also expressed the hope that the hijacking might in some way help concentrate people's minds on the nightmare of hostage-taking: 'Two years on and we seem to be no further on.' They were worried about the SAS storming the plane. 'That really terrified us – we knew that only sometimes they were successful – we knew that a lot of lives could be lost. We felt helpless, as if we were tied up in knots and couldn't move,' Elaine said. 'When talking to people from the plane afterwards, they said that they wished that the SAS wouldn't come in and that was all they were worrying about.' Brenda added: 'It was horrible. We never closed our eyes. I remember seeing the plane on TV and word coming through that they were not being given permission to land. I kept saying, "Please somebody let them come down." When the first body was thrown from the plane, it really killed me – I will never forget that thud on the tarmac. I felt for his family and what they must have been going through; we shared the same grief. Although death is a final thing and you finally come to live with it, you can't in a hostage situation.' The PLO leader, Yasser Arafat, said that he was willing to negotiate between the Kuwaitis and the hijackers. 'You knew that it was impossible to get inside their minds, which could change at any time,' Elaine said. 'When the PLO intervened with the hijack of the Kuwaiti airliner, we considered using the PLO to help us.' The hijack ended on 20 April. Two passengers had been shot dead in Cyprus during the ordeal.

Around the time of the second anniversary, the women decided to concentrate their energies on the Middle East and on the group holding Brian; they wanted to ensure that there would be at least a monthly mention of him in the Beirut press. They felt that this switch in direction was necessary to speed up things. Growing more knowledgeable about the type of people who were holding Brian, they realised that his captors thought about things in different ways to them. 'We were always trying to get somebody to come and say we have him – or he is alive or dead,' Brenda said. 'Looking back on it, we are happy that nobody did claim because then you would always have somebody to condemn.' They wrote a letter of appeal to the Beirut press. The sisters consulted their mother on almost every aspect of the campaign, but she was always concerned for the safety of those involved. The women also became more cautious and more aware of the right things to say. 'You thought deeper and had a lot of discussion before you acted.' Despite the situation, there were no times that they can recall when they regretted any appeals or statements they had made. 'The one thing that worried me,' Elaine said, 'was being on TV and not having my necklace tucked in. I wore the Star of David. I have no belief – it was bought for me and I just wore it. It was dangerous, but I just didn't think about it at the time. It is not something you think about at five o'clock in the morning, when you have to get up to do interviews.'

4

STRENGTH IN NUMBERS

Ireland's Minister for Foreign Affairs, Brian Lenihan, sat listening to the strange contingent from Belfast. It was 12 April 1988, a day after the second anniversary of Brian Keenan's kidnap. Elaine and Brenda were accompanied by Jim McIlwaine and Robert McGuckin. There was power in numbers, and the women felt strengthened when other members of the group attended these high-level meetings with government ministers. It was the first time that the women had met Brian Lenihan. 'The officials probably thought that they could manipulate us and that they could not do that if there was a man there. You could see Foreign Affairs thought that they could hoodwink us because we were two housewives, but when they saw that there was more strength there, things changed,' Elaine said.

Earlier that day, they had met officials from Foreign Affairs, but had found the discussions unsatisfactory. The sisters felt that Dublin believed that the main course of action should be the building of links with the Syrians and they were reluctant to put pressure on the Iranians. 'They argued the point with us. They said we should contact the Syrians, but not the Iranians,' Elaine said. When they were ushered in to Brian Lenihan's office, they put behind them those reports that said that their brother was dead. Any nerves and feelings of inferiority they had felt at previous meetings were abandoned during their short talk with Lenihan. Instead, they set out simply and directly their main requirement – more ministerial approaches to the Iranians. They also called for Irish political representatives to travel to Iran. Lenihan turned to his officials and told them to give the women what they wanted.

Brian Lenihan later revealed that there had been a 'general presumption' in his department that Keenan was dead: 'It was a general view which was held by the foreign affairs departments in London, Washington and Paris about all the hostages. It was very logical to presume that; there wasn't a whisper or a word out of Beirut. Everyone was coming up against a blank wall.' But he said that Brenda and Elaine spoke with complete certainty that their brother was alive. 'They had nothing hard to go on, yet they were so full of faith. They spoke with so much conviction that Brian was alive and I was convinced by that.'

For at least a year, very little happened about either of their demands. With the help of the campaign group, the sisters began to document the details of these meetings – there were about six in all. From then on, they discussed the Dublin meetings with their campaign group in Belfast and agreed a list of demands for action by the Irish government. As they became more acquainted with the volatile situation in Lebanon and other parts of the Middle East, their requirements became more specific. If officials asked them why they wanted a certain thing done, they knew how to reply because they had prepared an answer beforehand. They also decided to publicise any meeting they were attending in Dublin and often held a press conference afterwards. Frank Connolly, a Dublin-based freelance journalist, who had become involved in the campaign, always alerted the Irish papers, television and radio of an impending visit by the group.

He also co-ordinated meetings with interested parliamentarians, MEPs and senators.

Shortly after the second anniversary, the Irish government regularly placed advertisements in Lebanese newspapers in an effort to contact Keenan. They also had done this immediately after his kidnapping. On 4 May 1988, the French hostages, Jean-Paul Kauffmann, Marcel Fontaine and Marcel Carton, were released. They had been held by Islamic Jihad for three years.

Brenda watched their release with her two youngest children: 'Tears of joy were also something which you shared with the family. It was a joyous time when Kauffmann got out. It was the relief and that was before he [Kauffmann] said that Brian was alive,' Brenda said. Frozen assets owed by the French were paid to the Iranian government around the time of the releases. 'We always said that if we had it we would have given it,' Elaine said.

When the sisters raised the issue of a ransom payment with Foreign Affairs, they were told that the department would wait until the situation arose. It did several weeks later. The extorting of ransoms had become a homegrown industry in Ireland. Between 1975 and 1985, more than a dozen people, and Shergar, the most expensive racehorse in the world, were kidnapped in Ireland. Most took place in the Republic and, in more than half the cases, a ransom demand was paid.

First reports from Foreign Affairs indicated the French hostages had not mentioned Keenan, but the sisters were delighted that the three men had been freed. The release not only gave them hope that their brother would soon be liberated, it also relieved them because the three Frenchmen did not look too bad after their ordeal. Elaine said: 'Because these three

Frenchmen had been held for so long, it made you think that people could be held for years and still come out alive and looking all right.' A few days after the release, Jill Morrell saw Kauffmann in France; he told her that McCarthy and Keenan were alive and were being held together. The sisters were ecstatic when Jill phoned to tell them the news. It was the first positive word they had received in more than eighteen months.

They were also greatly comforted by the news that the two men were together. 'You were pleased because at least they had the company of each other. We knew that Brian could cope on his own because he was a strong-willed person, but as time went on, you wanted someone to be with him.' McCarthy had been in Beirut for only a month when he was kidnapped. He had been the acting head of Worldwide Television News's office in Beirut. A lively, outgoing man, he seemed to be a good match for Brian, and this was a solace to the sisters.

Kauffmann was interviewed by both Irish and British diplomats; he revealed more to the campaign groups at a later stage. Their perception of Iran's role in the release convinced the women that they had been correct in insisting that Dublin should make more approaches to Iran. It also made them think about bargaining for the release: 'There are many ways of doing deals – you can help the country and the people.'

The sisters met Jean-Paul Kauffmann in a London hotel six weeks after his release. The freed hostage was anxious to talk to them, but the language barrier proved to be difficult and, at times, frustrating. Jill Morrell, who had invited Kauffmann to London, had organised a translator for the meeting. Kauffmann told them that their brother was annoyed because he was being still thought of as British and that he had gone on hunger strike for a while to protest. The sisters shy away from the words 'hunger strike', preferring to say that Brian had refused to eat. 'We knew that Brian had the ability to do so because he was such a determined person.' Kauffmann knew little of the circumstances of Keenan's hunger strike because his information had been passed on by other hostages. On Kauffmann's instructions, none of what he told the sisters was divulged: 'He was very anxious to talk. He tried to get a lot out in a very short space of time. We also were afraid of pressurising him too much, but we had to speak to the man himself – that was very important. You also knew that he would say things to us that he would not tell to Foreign Affairs.' The women were relieved to see how well Kauffmann looked. 'We were consoled because we saw that life could go on after three years, and that gave us a lot of hope. We knew that the longer it went on there was the less chance of them killing Brian.'

The following day, Brenda travelled to Dublin for a meeting with an ad hoc group of supporters, including Tom Kitt, a Fianna Fáil TD, and Senator John Connor of Fine Gael. The meeting was designed to put as much pressure as possible on the Government. The politicians promised to make representations to the Taoiseach to try to intensify meetings with Iran. The women were amazed at the interest shown by the politicians, especially since Keenan was not one of their constituents. Such commitment was in marked contrast to the response of most Northern politicians. 'We were not sticking to one political party. It was good to have the support of both sides of the Dáil,' Brenda said.

During her two days in Dublin, Brenda met officials from Foreign Affairs and was told about the appointment of Khaled Daouk as Ireland's honorary consul in Beirut. A wealthy middle-aged Lebanese businessman, Daouk was an agent for An Bord Bainne (the Republic's milk marketing board) in Beirut. He would be formally appointed in the summer of 1988. According to diplomats in the Middle East, Daouk had good contacts throughout Lebanon, but at this stage he had uncovered nothing; some members of the group doubted that he would. About this time, Conor Murphy, a senior officer in the consular section of Foreign Affairs, started to telephone Brenda once a week. 'Sometimes we would only talk about things like the Iran–Iraq war. I felt that this was what was needed,' he said.

The sisters also discovered some important new information about Brian from a woman called Linda Keen, who had taught with him at the AUB. Linda, who had moved back to England, came to Belfast to visit the sisters. 'She could tell us things about Brian out there which we did not know before,' Brenda said. The night before he was kidnapped, Keenan had had dinner with Linda Keen. The meal was originally intended to be a celebration for him moving house. 'She told us that he always wore a notorious bright canary-yellow shirt and bright red braces and he was the talk of the university.' The meeting was also important because it gave the women a chance to ask her if Brian had done anything provocative before his kidnap. They were told that he had not.

At this time, there was a flurry of rumours about the hostages, one of which claimed that Terry Waite had seen Keenan shortly before he himself was kidnapped. This has never been proven. There was also speculation that the hostages were being moved to the Iranian embassy in Beirut or to the Bekaa Valley. The sisters were worried because they had heard of the ordeal hostages had to endure when they were being moved from one location to another. Irish peer Lord Kilbracken told a newspaper that he was going out to Iran to work on Brian's behalf. 'He seemed to be genuinely concerned, but he did not come back with any answer for us,' Brenda said. Several newspapers also reported at this time that three Britons would be released within four months. But the women paid little attention, saying that any report which includes a photograph of hostages must be treated with scepticism. 'We thought that in four months, we would have something anyway,' Elaine said.

The sisters were very pleased with the support they received at a rally in Cornmarket in Belfast city centre in June. One woman sticks out in Brenda's mind: 'I remember she was in a wheelchair. She asked could she sign the petition and she whispered that she was a Catholic and I told her that it did not matter what she was because we all believed in the same God. The tears were tripping me.'

There was one humorous moment that summer. Buzz Logan, a close friend of their brother's, whose photograph of Brian was used throughout the campaign, wrote to Brian. He had attended a lecture in Coleraine given by a Beirut-based expert on Lebanon. That night, he went home and wrote a letter addressed to the 'Irish Hostage, Hostage Hilton, Beirut', taking care to post it in Dublin. The letter never reached Keenan.

A local singer, Paul Herron, phoned the sisters and said he would like to write a song about Brian. Brenda supplied a poem that she had written about her brother and Herron composed the tune. The song includes the words: 'London doesn't worry much; he's just an Irishman./Dublin has been slow to move – is this a no-man's land?'

Mick's diary speaks about a 'breakthrough at last'. This was

in reaction to Charles Haughey's meeting with the Iranian foreign minister, Ali Akbar Velayati, at the United Nations. 'It was
Haughey doing the talking and he was the top man,' Elaine said.
'It was something we had been angling for, for a long time.
Whether the Irish had met the Iranians before or not I don't
know, and they were not going to tell us. They said that they
would do what they could.' It later transpired that Velayati
had not been aware of Keenan's case until Haughey had
mentioned it.

In the middle of July, Iran accepted the United Nations
Security Council resolution 598 for a ceasefire in its war with
Iraq. A few weeks later, a British diplomat, David Redaway,
made an official visit to Teheran. Because of a relaxing of
relations with Iran, the sisters decided that they wanted to visit
Teheran around the time of Brian's thirty-eighth birthday in
September. Michael D. Higgins encouraged them to go to
the Iranian capital. 'It would have been a good time to send
medical aid to Iran,' Elaine said. 'No government would have
seen it as a deal.' Brian's old friend from their nuclear
disarmament days, Terri Hooley, organised a special band to
raise funds for the trip. The campaign group wrote to other
bodies, asking them to join in an effort to get medical supplies
out to Iran but, according to the sisters, none were interested:
'Every group had to see to their own and they were occupied
with themselves.'

Ever since their meeting in the Iranian embassy in London in
December 1987, they had become very concerned about the
Iranian hostages being held in Beirut. 'We had seen or had been
in contact with the families of most of the other hostages,' Elaine
said. 'And we wanted to do the same for the Iranian ones. We

71

did not see why they should be excluded, because their suffering was the same as ours, no matter what their nationality.'

The women received little initial help from Foreign Affairs in their attempts to get to Iran: 'They tried to put us off, but when they realised that we were quite serious about wanting to go anyway, they did say that the Irish chargé d'affaires would see to us and would arrange accommodation.' But they seemed to be getting signals from diplomats and from Foreign Affairs: 'We were not sure about the reception they would get,' one official said. 'They were going into really deep water.' A diary entry on 8 September says that Patrick McCabe had been in touch; there was nothing new to convey, but he had said that a trip to Iran could be useful if they were to meet the right people. The women wanted to meet the Iranians informally: 'We wanted to see Rafsanjani as a family, not as one government to another,' Brenda made clear. 'The war was ending and when that happened, they had more on their plate than seeing us. We wanted to go from the beginning of the kidnap, but the government were never over-keen on it.' The sisters even went and had the necessary vaccinations for going to Iran.

In August, a statement from Islamic Jihad dashed some of their hopes of an early release. It said that the Americans Terry Anderson and Tom Sutherland would not be released until Israel had withdrawn its forces from southern Lebanon. They also demanded aid for the reconstruction of the area the Israelis had occupied and for the district populated by the Shia refugees in south Beirut.

In September, Niall Andrews, a Fianna Fáil MEP, received a phone call from the Iranian ambassador in Dublin, Bahram Ghassemi, asking him to come and meet him. Andrews, and his brother David, a Fianna Fáil TD, had been pushing for some time for a government delegation to go to Teheran, believing that the ceasefire could provide a valuable break in the hostage negotiations. The brothers thought that Iran wanted international recognition after the Iran–Iraq war. Niall Andrews, who had stayed in regular contact with Ghassemi, was also given a message to relay to the Keenan sisters. Ghassemi told them to hold off their visit to Teheran. He also assured Andrews that he intended to speak about Keenan during his next visit to Teheran. Interviewed by Kevin Dawson, a *Sunday Tribune* journalist, after Keenan's release, Ghassemi said that when initial enquiries were made in Lebanon, he could find out no information about the Irishman's whereabouts. For a while, he said, he got the impression that there was no Irish hostage.

In the September issue of the Dublin-based magazine *Magill*, a report said that some of the campaigners in the Friends of Brian Keenan Action Group were claiming that 'the lack of interest shown by the political establishment in the South is because of a suspicion which has been circulated in diplomatic circles that Keenan was in Beirut for purposes other than teaching English'. It maintained that the Irish government had been told about where Keenan was staying and said that top-level talks would be fruitful, adding that the Government had not acted on that information. Foreign Affairs was furious about this report. An official expressed concern that the 'other purposes' reference could cause suffering for Keenan and his family. 'It upset us very much. No allegations were made at all,' an official said. He contended that the family were immediately telephoned to allay any concerns that they may have had about the article.

Later that month, the sisters travelled to London to discuss coverage of the campaign with the BBC. While they were there, the BBC's foreign affairs editor, John Simpson, asked to see them. He told them that he believed that there might be a release in October. The sisters could not get home quickly enough to get their cases packed. 'I remember coming home and borrowing a suitcase and it sat there and sat there until we took the clothes out and started wearing them,' Elaine said. Nothing happened in October.

Meetings between the Irish government and the Iranians were stepped up towards the end of September. Brian Lenihan met Velayati at the United Nations in New York. The Iranian foreign minister told him that his government had received no information about Keenan. The next month, Lenihan met the Iranian ambassador to Ireland to discuss trade links. Keenan's case was raised. Ghassemi said that he was now aware of the facts and that he would be in contact with his colleagues in Iran. The sisters were also informed that Patrick McCabe had met Sheikh Fadlallah and Nabih Berri, but neither of them had any word about Keenan. Robert McGuckin assured them that Brian would be released before Christmas. A short time later, he told them to expect a letter from Brian, which would be addressed to his mother and would arrive at their aunt's house. No such letter arrived.

Keenan did write one letter exactly a year after his abduction. It was after a period when he had been formally interrogated by his captors over two days. Towards the end of the interrogation, he was twice offered the opportunity to write a letter, but he refused on both occasions. The letter he finally wrote was addressed to his mother's home with his friend Jim McIlwaine's name on the envelope. In a covering note, he instructed Jim to see that someone was with his mother when she read the letter. Keenan asked Jim to read the letter carefully. The family never received it. Five months later, he claims, he was at a different location and was brought a copy of the Lebanese newspaper *An-Nahar*, in which there was a letter, 'To the Irish Hostage', supposedly written by his family. Keenan noted that it contained three or four phrases that seemed to have been lifted from his letter to his mother. He believes that Foreign Affairs may have received the letter. An official said that they never got any such letter. 'We got absolutely nothing. Maybe it was a coincidence of drafting,' a senior official said.

Later that year, diplomatic relations between Iran and Britain were restored. The British embassy in Teheran was formally reopened on 9 December. Despite the fact that Keenan was carrying an Irish passport, the sisters say that they were pleased because the restoration of full diplomatic relations between Britain and Iran opened one more door for them.

Yet, just as things seemed to be picking up and improving on the diplomatic front towards the end of 1988, Elaine said that she was finding it increasingly hard to cope: 'I personally felt that my mind was completely confused and that I was not taking in anything. I found it very hard to have conversations with people. My mother often said that we were neglecting our children. You could see that the children were not dependent on us at all and that was hard to accept. I found that I could not cope when people all started talking at once. Stephen was wanting to sit down and listen and I did not have time in my own home to sit down and talk to him. Sometimes he reacted angrily, saying that all he was trying to do was to pull me back into reality. The more I explained to Stephen, the more confused I became. At times when it was right for Stephen to sit down and listen, it was not right for me to sit down and explain. He felt very much like an outsider in all that was going on and you had to keep reassuring him that he was not. There was no time together and no socialising together.' Most of the time was spent in Brenda's house. When Stephen would return to their home, there would often be news reporters and cameras there. Elaine said that she tried to cram into her head as much information about the Middle East as she possibly could. But she felt that her duty was in the home and she was frequently preparing meals for the freezer and washing clothes in case she was called away. 'Stephen and Mick were thrown into roles of both father and mother through no fault of their own.'

A few days before Christmas, the group held a candlelit vigil in Belfast. Jim McIlwaine recalls how another group member, Gerry McLaughlin, hit on the idea that they should use firelighters, which would be held inside wire cages during the vigil. Jim went round to Gerry's house and found that it had nearly been set on fire because of the experiment.

That week, the sisters were incensed when they read an interview with writer Gordon Thomas in the *Belfast Telegraph*. When he was asked about Brenda and Elaine, Thomas said: 'My advice to them would be to talk less to the world and trust those who are in touch with the situation.' They wanted to speak to him, but they never did. 'We were very, very angry about it. I wonder how he would feel if it had been his son or brother.'

In the New Year, Brian Lenihan had another meeting with Velayati in Paris. That same month, Brenda and Elaine flew to London for a secret meeting with the Anglican Primate of All

Ireland, Dr Robin Eames. They also met the Archbishop of Canterbury, Dr Robert Runcie, a Foreign Office official, and businessmen and clergy who had been in Lebanon. Dr Eames, who had met the women only a few months before, was struck by how down-to-earth they were, but he also says that they were very frightened: 'The most amazing thing was to hear Brenda talking about the politics of the Middle East. She knew far more about it than me.'

Brenda admits that she was terrified when she first met Dr Eames because she expected him to be as aloof as Dr Runcie, whom they had met briefly in London in January 1987. Dr Eames proved not to be and he became a supportive friend, staying in close touch with the women. 'He asked what church we were and I told him that it was Church of Ireland,' Brenda said. 'He said that he did not want to step on anyone's toes. He said that he would be willing to use any contacts he had. He asked me how did we think that Brian would have changed and I told him that we did not think that he would have.'

Dr Eames also expressed his concern about the Sinn Féin visit to Beirut. 'I could see his point,' Brenda said, 'because he can't get involved if we're mixed up with organisations. We weren't and I assured him of that. He was very direct. He also asked about Brian and we told him that he was not involved in any political organisations, but that he had friends who came from nationalist areas.' It was at that stage that the archbishop said that he would be happy to do something. 'He was the man at the top of our faith. He knew we were Protestants, but he had not known what church we were involved in.' The women thought that the Lambeth Palace connection was very important, but it was an aspect of the campaign that the Dublin bureaucrats always wanted to play down because they were concerned that Keenan would be identified with the British and especially with Terry Waite. Dr Eames waited for the first approaches to come from the women. From the start, he told them that there would be things that he might discover which he would not be able to communicate with them.

At the end of January 1989, the sisters travelled to Dublin and took part in a picket of the Dáil. This was one of a number of demonstrations taking place outside Leinster House because it was Budget Day. News started to break that Brian Keenan was about to be released. The women had planned to stay in Dublin for one night only. They ended up staying for three. That day, Khaled Daouk, Ireland's honorary consul in Beirut, telexed a message to Foreign Affairs saying that Keenan would be released in twenty-four hours. It is not known how the story started, but some say that it may have been sparked by the presence in Damascus of Declan Connolly, Ireland's ambassador to Syria. Connolly, who was mostly based in Riyadh in Saudi Arabia, was on a fairly routine visit to the Syrian capital, where he met senior officials in the Syrian foreign ministry and Dutch diplomats. For some years, the Dutch embassy had allowed the Irish to use its address to send and receive mail. Connolly's visit is believed to have aroused suspicions that he was in Damascus preparing for Keenan's release. The Department of Foreign Affairs told Patrick McCabe to find out everything he could in Beirut and he immediately travelled there from Baghdad.

Officers in Foreign Affairs were themselves unsure about whether the release was to take place, but they prepared an outline of what it would entail. They stress now that the finer points were not ironed out at the time. The women and campaign group

78

member Frank McCallan met Brian Lenihan. Minutes before the meeting, however, it was almost called off because officials were reluctant to allow McCallan, a forceful trade unionist, to see Lenihan. McCallan had taken part in the earlier demonstration outside Leinster House. The three made a pact that they would attend only if they were all allowed in. At the meeting with Lenihan, the sisters and McCallan urged that the Irish government give full recognition to the campaign group. They also asked for financial assistance to run an office in Belfast and to help print campaign leaflets. According to McCallan, Lenihan replied to the demands by saying that he did not involve himself in the intricacies of his departmental budget. He asked one of his officials to look into the matter. The campaign group was never provided with an office nor any of their other requests from that meeting. Later that day, a press officer told them that things were moving in Beirut and they were told to stay in Dublin. The sisters got the impression that the release might take about a week. 'That was the first time that someone in authority gave us a date.'

They walked back to their hotel and then went out for a meal. On their return, they went to bed, but did not get much sleep. Conor Murphy, from the consular section in Foreign Affairs, rang them and told them to get prepared. 'Conor Murphy was over the moon and you knew that he thought that this was it.' The women were short on cash and did not have a change of clothes. Frank McCallan and Joe Lenaghan, who had also taken part in the Dáil picket, stayed on in Dublin with them. Buswells Hotel, near Leinster House, where they were staying, was thronged with reporters. 'We never left our room. It was terrible. We ended up having to get into and leave the hotel by the back door.' At one point, the sisters returned to the hotel and were told that Iranian officials wanted to see them. The afternoon meeting had been arranged by Niall Andrews. They had been scheduled to meet Foreign Affairs officials, but decided to go instead to talk to the Iranians.

They met Ghassemi at the Iranian embassy in Blackrock, a Dublin suburb. Brenda remembers being scared that she was going to get stuck in the electronic gate at the entrance. The sisters were hopeful that this meeting would be a precursor to Brian's release. They told the ambassador about the reports that were coming through, but he said that they had heard nothing. He stressed yet again that there was a mix-up over their brother's nationality. He said that he would do all he could and asked them to speak out on behalf of the Iranian hostages being held in Lebanon. When the sisters told him how they were being hounded by the media, he said that they could use the embassy as their second home.

At four o'clock, they returned to the hotel where they were telephoned by Foreign Affairs to say that everything was dying down. Brenda took the phone call and was bitterly disappointed when she heard the news. She shouted down the phone and, afterwards, was unable to speak. The rest of the campaign group knew the reason for her anger. They had booked a room in the hotel for a press conference that was due to start at 4.30. Brenda was so distressed that she could not face the reporters and cameras. 'The whole build-up and the meeting with the Iranians was nerve-wracking. All these reporters around us were telling us that he was getting out. I just felt as if my mind had blown and I thought, How could they do this to us? Joe made me lie down. The group was rough and ready but in times like that, they were brilliant.'

Elaine was enraged at the lack of help and support from Foreign Affairs: 'We were so annoyed that they sat around in their cushy Foreign Affairs offices and did not release a press statement saying that it was over. They must have known the pressures that we were going through.' But officials maintain that they did not believe that hopes of a release were forlorn.

Elaine spoke at the press conference. Frank McCallan helped her down the stairs. 'It was very, very frightening and I knew by Frank's protection that we would be in for a rough time. I told Brenda that we had to do the press conference.' In the past, the women had needed the press to publicise their plight, and they appreciated what they had done, but they increasingly felt that other members of the group should act as spokespeople. Yet, according to Joe Lenaghan, the media rarely wanted to speak to anyone but the sisters.

Elaine was not prepared for the press conference. The bad news they had just received had not sunk in. She broke down during it. 'I was very nervous, more so than normal and I could not hide it. I knew that everything was crumbling, I thought that I was not capable of leaving that room. I just wanted to get away from everybody, but you could not have gone an inch either way because you were surrounded. When I cried, it was not because of Brian not getting out, but because my mind was suffocated and the reporters were looking for answers which I could not give them.' Elaine believes now that she let herself down at the press conference. She was trembling so much that she could not take a drink of water. 'You are so worried about this image for Stephen and Ashleigh in Belfast which comes across on the television.' She also implored the assembled reporters not to hype up the hostage situation any more than it was already.

81

Before the party left for Belfast, they had to borrow money to pay the hotel bill. The press did not believe what Elaine had told them and suspected that an Irish government plane was on standby. The campaign group's car was followed by reporters as far as Dublin airport on its way back to Belfast. The return journey was very painful and for the first time their homes felt like empty shells: 'There was no meaning to the home. You had to go back and face those children and you could see the questioning in their eyes and you wish that you could answer their questions,' Brenda said.

Elaine said that when they were away, their partners lived for the television: 'Watching the Dublin press conference did not provide them with a pleasant sight. It was the first time that Stephen had seen me crack up. He did not want to know the ins and outs like other occasions. I think he thought that it was the final straw with me.' Stephen advised her to go to their doctor. Every time the sisters visited their doctor during the four and a half years, they were told that they must be suffering from stress. 'If they had given me something to knock me out, it would not have worked,' Elaine said. 'I suffered from headaches, which really drained me and you wanted to be alone, but also you wanted someone there. It's hard to take when people say that you are neglecting this and that, but you don't see it and then it's too late. Sometimes when you went to the doctor, you would rather if they told you that you only had six months to live rather than them telling you that you were the sister of a hostage.' After that, Elaine often pulled the phone out of the wall to ensure that reporters could not reach her. 'When you come home, you have to relive it. I used to make dinner for everyone but myself. It would have been great just to sit down and have a Sunday dinner after a week's work. It just did not happen.'

Brenda was glad to get back to the security of her family, but she still felt ill: 'We were both really sick for about a week afterwards and I think that it was all nerves, particularly reaching the Iranians in Dublin for the first time. When you look back, you see how much you put yourself through, but we knew that if we stopped the world would stop.' Both women learnt a lot from the experience and agreed that if a similar situation reoccurred, they would handle the media very differently.

The sisters continued to see reports of the Irish diplomatic efforts in the Middle East, but the initiative slowly died a death. Patrick McCabe stayed in Beirut for three weeks and tried contact after contact. He did manage to unearth some people with Hezbollah links, including a doctor, whom Daouk had recommended he should see. The doctor had attended the CIA man, William Buckley, whose kidnapping had been claimed by Islamic Jihad. Buckley died under torture in June 1985.

Dr Eames phoned the sisters on 8 February and said that he had heard from two separate sources that Brian was still alive, but that there was no imminent prospect of a release. Foreign Affairs then told the sisters that Brian Lenihan was going to Iran in April; they were advised to keep the news to themselves. Niall Andrews also flew to Iran in February and returned convinced that the hostages were all still alive.

But suddenly all hopes were dashed. The 18 February entry in Mick's diary reads: 'A book by the author Salman Rushdie, who was brought up as a Muslim, has wrecked all chances of a release in the near future. In this book he blasphemes the Muslim religion and Mohammed.' Four days earlier, Ayatollah

Khomeini had called for Rushdie's death because of so-called blasphemies in his novel *The Satanic Verses*, first published in the United Kingdom the previous September. Muslim communities throughout the world considered the book to be an insult to Islam. The Ayatollah's *fatwa* caused a diplomatic row which wrecked the improving relations between Iran and Britain. It was a very worrying time for the women: 'Salman Rushdie was brought up a Muslim,' Brenda said, 'and he should have known better. We can understand the Muslim people fighting back, but we never accepted the death threat. Christian people do not like a mockery being made of Jesus Christ.'

Less than a week later, the European Community (EC) decided to withdraw its top diplomats from Teheran and agreed to suspend high-level visits to Iran in protest against the death threat. The Hezbollah spiritual leader, Sheikh Fadlallah, said that the diplomatic offensive might induce Iran to postpone its efforts on behalf of the hostages. 'Our worry first was that it would affect the British hostages because Brian was sometimes being portrayed as British,' Brenda said. Ireland did not close down its embassy in Teheran nor did it expel Iranian diplomats from Dublin.

When the sisters phoned Foreign Affairs, officials told them not to worry, adding that all its staff would be back in the Iranian capital shortly. They were also warned not to give interviews on the subject, but they did prepare a statement. Believing that a paperback edition of *The Satanic Verses* would cause further friction and threats to the hostages, the sisters signed a petition calling for the paperback not to be published. In March, they were told that a source in the Amal had said that, two weeks before, Brian had been made ready for release. At the end of

February, according to the report, he was shaved, and was given a haircut and new clothes. This has proven to be untrue.

During a Hezbollah-organised protest in Beirut, attended by 5,000 Muslims, an effigy of Rushdie was burnt. The sisters were considerably relieved, however, when the Irish chargé d'affaires, Noel O'Byrne, returned to Teheran on 30 March. Ireland was one of the first countries to reopen full diplomatic relations with Iran.

5

WIDENING THE CIRCLE

A handful of people stood bearing placards in the pouring rain outside Leinster House on the morning of 11 April 1989. It was the third anniversary of Brian Keenan's kidnap and the campaign group had decided to concentrate more of its activities in Dublin, the entrance gates to Ireland's parliament becoming a replacement for Belfast city centre. In contrast to Belfast, the group found that most of the politicians entering the Dáil were stopping to express their support. Basing the main protest for the anniversary in Dublin was a significant step. The women and their ever-strengthening campaign group were anxious to put considerable pressure on the Irish government, and what better time to do it than on the anniversary of their brother's abduction. In the Republic, people were becoming more aware of Keenan's plight, while the sisters felt that the Belfast public was growing tired of their frequent appearances on television: 'The people of Belfast had seen us all the time for three years and I'm sure they were sick of us.'

A woman approached them outside Leinster House. She told the sisters that she had been a nun and that she wanted to convey a message to them from God: their brother would come home only when Elaine and Brenda started talking about a united Ireland. They did not engage her in debate and now laugh about the incident. 'The last thing for us would have been talking about a united Ireland. We would have been dead before he got out,' Elaine said.

Later that day, they met Foreign Affairs officials and Seán Calleary, the minister of state who was standing in because Brian Lenihan was ill at the time. Lenihan had collapsed and medical advisers decided that he should be rushed to the Mayo Clinic in the United States for a kidney transplant. The group left the meeting believing that Calleary was interested in the case, but they also knew that he was not the minister. He promised to do all he could to help them. They were pressing for approaches to be made to Colonel Gaddafi and to the PLO and said that they would travel to Libya to meet Gaddafi if need be. 'We were not asking anyone else to talk to him. No one would have to be accused of doing deals with terrorists.' The sisters were impressed and heartened at the growing level of activity in Dublin. Western relations with Iran were still suffering and were severely complicated by the Salman Rushdie affair. According to Foreign Affairs, it lasted for a year, during which intensive efforts were made to break the diplomatic deadlock. The campaign group was still insistent that direct political approaches be made to Iran itself rather than at ambassadorial level. 'How long did we shout about a delegation to Iran?' Elaine said. 'We did not want an ambassador going from Iraq to Iran, but someone going out from Ireland to Iran, and it took us a very long time to get that.' They were supported in their efforts to get to Teheran by Dáil deputies like Tom Kitt and David Andrews, who told them that they intended to meet the Taoiseach to persuade him to give the thumbs-up for a trip to Teheran.

But life in Beirut continued to be volatile and dangerous. A few days after the third anniversary, an editorial in *An-Nahar* was headed 'Lebanon's Apocalypse Continues'. At least forty-five people were killed when shells hit Western and Arab embassies, schools, universities and hospitals. The city was often without water and electricity.

Towards the end of April, the sisters received a phone call from Noel O'Byrne, who had been to see Iranian Foreign Affairs. They wanted to assure him that they were doing all they could for Keenan. Direct contact with such highly placed diplomats was unusual and the sisters greatly appreciated it. They were hopeful that Dr Eames would help secure their brother's release. He points out now that the Irish government was always keen that he should use his 'Primate of All Ireland' title because some people might construe his 'Anglican Archbishop' rubric as being too closely linked with Lambeth Palace. Brenda and Elaine were grateful to have close links with a senior Protestant clergyman: 'It let people see what we were and it showed that he was doing something to help us. Maybe then, it showed people that we were not the ones they thought we were.' Dr Eames had told them earlier that year that Brian was alive. According to his source, which he said was 'very good indeed', Brian had been a little unwell, but he had recovered.

At the end of April, Dr Eames addressed a church conference and appealed for Brian Keenan's release. His speech was very important for the women. He told the conference that Keenan was not mixed up in any political intrigue and was innocent of any crimes. 'When Dr Eames came on the scene, it was because he was fighting for a human being and not someone who was a republican or someone else from east Belfast,' Brenda said. A few weeks later, Dr Eames talked to the head of the Cypriot church and the Greek Orthodox church, who agreed to help. A fortnight later, the sisters received a note from Dr Eames to say that he had heard through a Syrian security chief that Brian and John McCarthy were still alive.

In May, Foreign Affairs told the sisters that Khaled Daouk, Ireland's honorary consul in Beirut, had been approached by someone about a ransom for Brian. It is believed that he also received another ransom demand during the kidnap. Daouk was visiting some of his family in Canada when a man approached his secretary who, in turn, rang Patrick McCabe. Foreign Affairs phoned Daouk in Canada and he returned at once to Lebanon. The man turned up a second time to see Daouk, demanding £4 million for Keenan's release. Daouk sent him away with a Bord Bainne sticker and told him to come back with a photograph of the sticker on Keenan's forehead. The man never returned. Some members of the campaign group believe that Daouk handled the incident badly. Frank McCallan thinks that he should have done more to establish the man's identity. According to Foreign Affairs, the man was not prepared to talk to Daouk.

It was another frustrating time for the sisters. 'No one ever gave names of the sources and that got you very angry,' Brenda said. 'People had at that stage grown to trust you and it would have helped us because we would have gone to them ourselves. You were hanging on the edge waiting for someone to come forward.'

Later that month, David Andrews and a Fianna Fáil senator, Mick Lanigan, met Colonel Gaddafi during a five-day visit to Libya. Their discussions were primarily about improving trade links between Ireland and Libya, but they told Gaddafi that they denounced anyone who supported violence. 'We told him that any person who was sending arms to Ireland was not a friend of Ireland's,' David Andrews said. The two men also broached the subject of Brian Keenan. Despite the fact that it was unlikely that Gaddafi had any great influence over the hostage-taking groups, he said that he would give whatever help he could. Clutching at all straws, Andrews told Gaddafi that Keenan had been offered a job in Libya before he had taken up his post in Beirut. Andrews, who had campaigned for the release of the Birmingham Six and the Guildford Four, was worried that the Keenan case would disappear from the public eye: 'It always concerned me that Brian Keenan was languishing in Beirut and his case could go off the boil for months. It was so important to keep up the level of public awareness.'

At the beginning of June, Ayatollah Khomeini died and Ali Khameni was elected temporarily to succeed him. Interviewed shortly afterwards, the sisters expressed mixed feelings about the caretaker president, saying that they were not sure about his attitudes towards the West. Their hope was that Rafsanjani, the more pragmatic and Westward-looking speaker of the Iranian parliament, would take over. Early that month, Rafsanjani said that it was up to Britain to solve the hostage affair and up to the United States to make serious attempts to help in the release of their citizens who were being held. Even speaking about the hostages was a significant advance because Ayatollah Khomeini had spoken of little else but the Islamisation of the world. Dublin said that Rafsanjani's statement was 'music to our ears'. He was elected president of Iran on 28 July and declared his determination to end his country's isolation.

Any optimism the sisters felt about Rafsanjani was short-lived because, on the day of his election, Israeli commandos abducted

Sheikh Abdul Karim Obeid, a spiritual leader of Hezbollah, from his home in southern Lebanon. Israel claimed that this action would help to break the deadlock in the hostage negotiations and demanded the freedom of three Israeli servicemen captured in southern Lebanon three years earlier. It then suggested that they would trade Obeid and 150 Lebanese Shias being held hostage in an Israeli jail in southern Lebanon, not just for their own servicemen but also for the Western hostages. Shortly after the Obeid kidnap, a videotape was released showing the apparent hanging of American hostage Lieutenant Colonel William Higgins. The Revolutionary Justice Organisation threatened to kill another American hostage, Joseph Cicippio, but Rafsanjani is understood to have prevented this. Four days after the Obeid kidnap, the Organisation of Oppressed on Earth threatened to kill Terry Waite. Foreign Affairs officials were very concerned about Keenan, but told the sisters that their brother was not in immediate danger. The department issued a statement condemning Israel for the kidnapping of Sheikh Obeid.

For the first weeks of the Obeid kidnap, the women never turned off their television sets. The worsening situation unfurled before them in their living rooms. They watched Cicippio's emotional plea for the release of Obeid. On 4 August, United States warships were ready for action off the Lebanese coast, but the threat subsided with Cicippio's reprieve. 'We knew that the slightest thing could destroy all lives. Americans loved to be the guys in the big picture, and it wasn't just their own hostages but all others,' Elaine said.

A week after Obeid had been kidnapped, Rafsanjani, at a prayer meeting in Teheran, told the White House that there was a solution for freeing the hostages: 'Take a sensible attitude and we will help solve the problems there [Lebanon] so the people of the region may live in peace and friendship.' On the same day, Sheikh Fadlallah made an unprecedented appeal to the hostage-takers, telling them not to harm their captives. Shortly afterwards, another Hezbollah leader, Hussein Musawi, admitted that his organisation knew some of the kidnappers of the hostages and said that Hezbollah had occasional meetings with the abductors. This was Hezbollah's first public acknowledgement of any involvement in the hostage crisis.

The summer of 1989 was one of great sadness for the sisters. On 8 July, John McCarthy's mother, Sheila, died of cancer. Two weeks earlier, she had issued an appeal to her son's kidnappers through her doctor, saying that her dying wish was to see him once more. It was a difficult time for their own mother too: 'We saw this poor woman on her death bed pleading. Sub-consciously, Mum thought that the same could happen her.' The following month, Keenan's close friend, Buzz Logan, died. A former photographer with the *Irish Independent*, Buzz Logan had started a project with Brian to set up a number of darkrooms in community centres throughout Belfast. Several still survive.

After Ireland's general election on 15 June, Gerard Collins of Fianna Fáil was appointed Minister for Foreign Affairs on 12 July. As soon as he took up his post, he was urged by the campaign group to go to Teheran to speak with the Iranian government. Brian Lenihan had promised to go there before he became ill. In July, the Irish became part of the EC troika, where the outgoing, incoming and incumbent of the EC presidency jointly assume responsibility for matters of foreign affairs. Ireland took up the post of EC president at the start of 1990.

From the beginning of the troika, the Irish played an active role in persuading their fellow member states to remove the EC embargo on trade with Iran and to consolidate relations with the new regime. On 7 September, Brenda, Joe Lenaghan and Frank Connolly met the new minister in Dublin. Joe Lenaghan was particularly impressed with Collins: 'You could see the different attitude that he was adopting. He was prepared to take our proposals, explore different avenues and give instructions to his senior officials. He made sure that they reported back to him.'

A few days after Brenda's visit to Dublin, Collins addressed a meeting of Arab and European parliamentarians in Dublin and told them that one of his priorities would be the revival of Arab-European dialogue. Lebanon and Libya were represented at this meeting.

Towards the end of September, Collins met the Iranian foreign minister, Ali Akbar Velayati, the Syrian foreign minister, Farouk Al-Shara, and their Algerian counterpart, Sid Ahmed Jhozali, at the United Nations General Assembly in New York. He also met representatives of the PLO. Foreign Affairs regarded these meetings as very important. Although the meetings were not yielding immediate results, they were 'getting the message through to the people who were watching that the machine was being kept constantly oiled,' one official said later. Collins also travelled to Washington where he met top officials from the State Department in the White House. Despite the significance of such meetings, the campaign group thought that the most important discussions should be held at ministerial level in Teheran. The group, which had become more politicised and more specific in its demands, believed that if Collins were to go to Iran for talks, it would help dispel the isolated image that country had had with the West since its revolution in 1978.

In October, Dr Eames phoned Brenda to say that one of his contacts in Cyprus wanted the family to put forward two questions that could be asked of Brian. They needed to be ones to which only he knew the answers. They suggested the first names of his parents and the name of his dog. They never heard any more about the matter. Dr Eames also asked if they would like to go to Cyprus for an Anglican conference the following January. The sisters said yes.

Towards the end of the year, various politicians in the Republic were mentioning Brian Keenan at every available opportunity during their increasing number of international meetings because Ireland was soon to take up the EC presidency. David Andrews continually raised his case in the Dáil. Gerard Collins met Yasser Arafat in Tunisia and the Syrians and Lebanese in Paris at a meeting of the Arab League. In November, Antoin Mac Unfraidh, former head of Middle East section, took over from Patrick McCabe as ambassador in Iraq.

Some of the diplomatic moves were happening through the Iranian embassy in Dublin. In late 1989, Bahram Ghassemi had discussions with Seán Calleary, the Minister of State at Foreign Affairs. He told Calleary that his country would be keen to establish a link with the EC and wondered if the Irish could facilitate them in any way. It was widely believed that all available opportunities should be grasped to try and rebuild relations with Iran.

A few days before Christmas, the campaign held a vigil at Belfast City Hall; it was attended by children from youth clubs that straddled the sectarian divide. The vigil made a lasting impression on the sisters. A short time before it took place, Brenda and Elaine decided to explain to the children what it meant to be a hostage. They were taken aback when the children started to ask questions. 'They asked us did we send food parcels and how many visits we got. They were talking about prison. For so many of them, this seemed to be their experience. You could have sat down and cried for them.'

In the New Year, Elaine and Brenda visited Cyprus where Dr Eames was addressing the provincial conference of Anglican bishops and clergy. They told the press that they were going away on holiday, but they were found out after a few days. Bishops and clergymen from all over the world attended the conference.

Dr Eames remembers watching the sisters one evening in Larnaca: 'They were sitting looking across at Beirut and all they could hear was shells.' He said that the women sat staring across the 100 miles of water towards Beirut for a very long time. At one point, the archbishop was fearful that they would board a ferry for Beirut while he was at the conference. Dr Eames said that if they did, it would not be his responsibility. Plans for their trip were almost complete when they got a phone call from Dr Eames saying that a community leader wanted to meet them. They believe that this meeting practically saved their lives because that day was a particularly violent one in east Beirut where their ferry would have landed.

But their meeting with the community leader, whose identity Dr Eames is reluctant to disclose, was to be one of the most important during their brother's long captivity. He told them that he lived above a Hezbollah group in Beirut and gave them information about Brian's health. He said that their brother had trouble with his teeth and his ears and that he had once seen a doctor. This information proved to be correct. Brian says that he had chronic pains in his ears and even went deaf for a while. He did see a doctor during his first year in captivity. The community leader asked if Brian needed any medication and assured the sisters that the hostages were seen regularly by doctors. But the sisters used the meeting to pass on a piece of important information: 'It was the only way that we could get word into Beirut that Brian was a bleeder because his blood had difficulty in clotting. We could not have put that into any of our appeals because the media would have picked up on it and made a bigger story out of it. We knew that the man could take it into Beirut.' The sisters went to see the PLO in Nicosia in Cyprus. The Palestinians told them that they had telegrammed Beirut for news of Brian. His sisters simply asked for evidence that he was alive. 'It was important to use everyone that you could and they had people on the ground there.'

February 1990 was a very quiet month with little or no developments. In the Middle Eastern press, there were some confusing signals about the hostage situation. On 22 February, the *Teheran Times* called for the unconditional release of all hostages. In an editorial, this English-language newspaper said: 'Regardless of the West's propaganda ploys, Muslim forces, out of Islamic and humanitarian considerations, should work to get the hostages free with no precondition.' A fortnight later, however, the Beirut newspaper *An-Nahar* quoted unidentified Lebanese fundamentalist sources as ruling out any quick release of the hostages. In March, the Minister of State at the Department of Defence, Vincent Brady, was in Lebanon for four days, visiting the UNIFIL contingent. He travelled to Damascus where he got an assurance from the Syrian defence minister, General Mustafa

Tlass, that Keenan was alive and well. Brady raised the case with the Lebanese defence minister Albert Mansour in Beirut. Brady rang the sisters to tell them what he had heard. But days later, a much more significant meeting took place in Dublin. On 22 March, the Iranian ambassador paid a visit to the Taoiseach, Charles Haughey. Such a call was a fairly unusual occurrence. Ghassemi made it clear that Keenan was alive. There was nothing explicit about his approach, but it was hopeful. He told Haughey that he was getting the Iranian embassy in Beirut to look into Keenan's case. It is still not known if Teheran had instructed its ambassador to arrange this meeting or whether the ambassador went to see Haughey off his own bat.

The following day, the Taoiseach sent Conor Murphy, from the consular section, to Belfast. It was the first time in almost four years that a Dublin-based public servant had met the sisters in Belfast. They talked in the Europa Hotel. Brenda could not believe it when Murphy told her over the phone he was on his way to Belfast: 'We knew something was in the air,' she said. Murphy told them that their brother was alive and he hoped that he would be released very soon. No one mentioned this meeting to the media. 'Foreign Affairs started to trust us enough to let us in on these things. If we had told the media, we would never have been trusted again.'

As the year progressed, the sisters' efforts to free their brother gained considerable momentum. 'The first two years nothing happened and then people started doing things and you heard reports all the time.' On the fourth anniversary of Brian Keenan's kidnap, Charles Haughey visited Belfast to address a meeting of the Institute of Directors in the Europa Hotel. It was the first official visit to Northern Ireland by a Taoiseach since 1965 when Seán Lemass had met the then Northern Ireland prime minister, Captain Terence O'Neill. Days before, the unionists, still protesting against the Anglo-Irish Agreement, were raising hell about the meeting. On the day itself, about 400 protesters, including the leader of the Democratic Unionist Party, the Reverend Ian Paisley, took over a main street outside the hotel to stage their demonstration. Speaking to the *Irish Times* about Charles Haughey, Dr Paisley said: 'I don't want to breathe the air he breathes.' The women had been scheduled to meet Haughey in the Europa on the day of the anniversary, but this meeting was cancelled. Foreign Affairs officials thought that a cancellation was sensible because of the disturbance, although plans had been made to sneak the women in through a back door of the hotel. Their vigil, to mark Brian Keenan's four years of captivity, went ahead in the relative tranquility of Cornmarket. The next day, the sisters received a postcard asking for money from someone in Belfast who offered help in Brian's release. Copies of the postcard were immediately passed on to Dr Eames and Haughey.

On 24 April, Gerard Collins had a forty-five-minute meeting with Ali Akbar Velayati at the United Nations in New York and was told that 'the Irishman would be freed'. At a previous meeting between the Iranian and Irish foreign ministers, Keenan's name was mentioned to Velayati and he had to ask what his Irish counterpart was talking about. 'Before then, he did not know who Brian Keenan was and now he was talking about him, saying his name.' Collins informed the sisters through his officials that no concessions had been asked for during the meeting. 'Even if he had asked, Foreign Affairs would not tell us. Until this day we don't know what got Brian out.'

The best news so far was about to happen. On 28 April, the American Frank Reed was released. The director of the Lebanese International School had been kidnapped on 9 September 1986. The women had no idea how much information Reed was going to be able to give them about their brother. 'We thought we would get something from Reed, but not as much as we did get.' Three days later, Pat O'Connor, a senior official who is head of the administration section at Foreign Affairs, rang them late at night and told them that Reed had seen their brother several days earlier. They were instructed to keep the news quiet. The following morning, Brenda's home was taken over by the media. Most of the press, radio and television interviews were conducted in her home, she says, because if they moved outside, they were guaranteed to attract a crowd of children.

Frank Reed, who had been moved to the US base in Wiesbaden, West Germany, was due to phone them at 3 pm, but he did not ring until after midnight. 'You tried not to get too high,' Elaine said, 'but the media made it worse and you ended up trying to control them. There was no room for us in our own home and we stayed out in the garden.' She took the phone call. 'Frank spoke as if he had known us for years and you can see why. He said Brian was OK and physically fit and better than he ever was. He also said that John [McCarthy] was alive and well. He told us about how Brian shouted continually about being Irish and about the bottles of Black Bush. Through it all, he [Reed] was swearing constantly and talking very quickly. He didn't tell us very much, apart from the fact that Brian was alive. He did say that the Syrians would be very important and that he would do everything he could to help us.'

Two days later, Reed phoned again and told the sisters that

he wanted to see them in the United States. They rang the Irish government to find out if they were going to send someone to talk to Reed. They were told that the Irish were having problems getting in touch with the Americans by telephone. But Pat O'Connor rang them and told them to get ready for a trip to the United States. Elaine maintains that the Foreign Affairs officials were going to use them to gain access to Reed: 'We were going to get them in quicker than they would get in themselves.' Officials say that when they tried to make contact with Reed in Wiesbaden, he was preparing to travel back to the United States. At the same time, Brenda and Elaine were packing their bags for their first and only trip to America.

6

FLESH AND BLOOD

After more than four years, Brenda and Elaine had grown tired
of living on rumours and reports from unnamed sources. They
wanted to see, hear and touch the man who had been with their
brother only a few days before. Foreign Affairs quickly acceded
to their demand to go and see Reed. Any previous worry the
sisters felt about going to the United States was dispelled. At
the end of 1986, for example, they were dissuaded from
attending a church service in Washington for a former hostage.
Their advisers in Foreign Affairs believed that it would be
prudent for them not to be seen going to the United States, one
of the main aggressors in the Middle East.

They made the decision to go immediately. It was arranged
that they would meet Frank Reed at Andrews Airforce Base on
5 May. They were accompanied by Frank McCallan. The Irish
ambassador, Padraic MacKernan, met them at Washington
airport.

The only time they had seen Frank Reed was on television, in
a dressing gown on the hospital balcony in Wiesbaden. When
they walked into the airforce base's medical centre, the
sisters were not prepared for the shock of seeing him. They met
Reed in a small lounge, off the hospital ward. He looked
pathetically thin, particularly when dressed in his ordinary
clothes. 'Brenda and I burst out crying and he told us that he
knew that we were sisters,' Elaine said. When the sisters had

met French hostages, Kauffmann and Rochot, there had been a language barrier.

Reed kept little back from the women and gave them some idea of the brutality of his captors. He said that when the hostages did something of which their guards disapproved, their blankets would be confiscated, even in wintertime. He told them that in the cell he had been last held in, Brian and John were chained to one wall; when they lay down, they were head to head. He was chained to another wall. Tom Sutherland and Terry Anderson were also held there. Reed told them that, at various times, he had been held in apartments. He had been held with Brian and John for the last six months. Conditions had improved and the guards were friendlier. Reed told them that their brother had been beaten several times. On one occasion, Brian was chained and lying facing a wall. When a guard came along, Brian had kicked out at him.

Reed said that Brian had a good personality and that they all played games with each other. They made a deck of cards and a chess set, which fitted into a matchbox. Brian always shouted out to his guards that he was not British and that he wanted to be handed over to Irish officials. Reed told them that Brian was holding up well and was dreaming of the pig farm he wanted to open when he got home. They also heard that he had received a letter. The hostages were given antibiotics. They each got five cigarettes a day. John and Brian shared theirs and, as a result, they constantly had the flu because they picked up infections from one another. The hostages were also given radios and had televisions for two weeks, as well as books and encyclopaedias. He did not know where the two men were currently being held, but he knew that there was a mosque close by. The women slowly began recognising details about the brother they had not seen for so long. Brian had introduced his fellow inmates to the wit of Northern Ireland, cracking jokes about Paisley and the Pope. At times, he and John would pretend to be Thatcher and Haughey in the throes of Anglo-Irish talks.

Speaking about his own release, Reed said that he had thought that he was the last American to be freed. He had been given trousers, a shirt, a tie, a pen and a watch. He thought that Brian and John were in the car behind him the whole way to Damascus, where he was brought after his release. He said that the authorities holding them knew about the beatings, but it is unlikely that they had ordered them. Reed warned those standing around him that the kidnappers wanted to talk and that if this did not happen, there would be trouble. Later, at the press conference, Elaine, Brenda and Frank were scared about what Reed was going to say, particularly when he mentioned Hezbollah. 'It was good to even know the worst about the hostages. You saw many of them coming out, but this was flesh and blood with his arms around you,' Brenda said. One quote from Reed struck a chord with both of the sisters: 'We simply don't want hostage-taking again. People have to control politicians, not the politicians controlling the people.' Brenda said: 'In the North, our own politicians did not really want to know.' Reed told them privately of his own psychological problems while he was in captivity: 'He did say that there were times when he knew that he was going a bit mad and that Brian was very worried about this.' During their two-hour meeting, Reed once confused Brian with John McCarthy, when he said that their brother was carrying a British passport. Reed also made unrealistic suggestions, such as his call for the Irish UNIFIL troops to be withdrawn from Lebanon.

On their return to Dublin, Foreign Affairs told them that diplomats would be sent out to Beirut as quickly as possible. For most of the rest of May, there was some quickening of pace on the political front. Normal relations between Iran and the EC were restored after more than a year of delicate negotiations. The Irish proposed to their fellow member states that there should be regular meetings with the Iranians. In the middle of May, a significant development towards the warming of relations with Iran took place when some of its top foreign ministry officials met the EC troika – their Irish, French and Italian counterparts – in Dublin. This was the first time that such a meeting had taken place and it was regarded as very important because it was Iran's attempt to rebuild fractured relations with the EC. The Iranians requested the meeting after intense negotiations by the Irish. A few days later, Antoin Mac Unfraidh told Sheikh Fadlallah that Keenan's decision to take an Irish passport was a 'political act'. Keenan, he said, could pick which passport he wished to be identified with and he had chosen an Irish one.

This was the latest in a long line of attempts to persuade people of influence in the Middle East about Keenan's identity. The fact of his Irishness took a long time for leaders like Fadlallah to grasp. Foreign Affairs continually stressed Ireland's neutrality and its peaceful demeanour towards other countries, but there was still a strange lack of appreciation of this. Having dual citizenship, as Keenan did, did not seem to be understood in the Middle East. And there was still concern in Dublin about the confusion over Keenan's nationality. At one point Pat

O'Connor told the sisters that Brian was more Irish than he was. 'When people asked us about the passport, we said that it was Brian's choice. At the start we did not know that he was on an Irish passport,' Elaine said.

In mid-June 1990, three Irish politicians travelled to Iran to emphasise the point about Keenan's nationality. The delegation, David and Niall Andrews and Senator Eoin Ryan, made a five-day trip to Teheran. They had been pressing for the visit for some time. According to Niall Andrews, when his brother David mentioned the trip to Collins, the minister had advised against it. The visit is believed to have been arranged largely with the help of the Iranian embassy in Dublin; Niall Andrews had been in close and regular contact with Ambassador Ghassemi for several years.

This trip has been acknowledged as important for several reasons. The three men were the first Western parliamentarians to visit Iran since the 1978 revolution. They played a crucial role in some of the first steps towards the non-isolation of Iran from the West and, by so doing, put more pressure on the Irish government to send an official delegation to Teheran. Iran had been looking for more recognition, especially from the EC, since the ending of its war with Iraq.

While they were in Teheran, the three parliamentarians met the deputy foreign minister, Mahmoud Vaezi, a senior official in the Iranian foreign ministry, Hussein Moussavian, and Said Ali Radjai Khorassani, the chairman of the foreign relations committee. David Andrews says that the delegation would have met Hashemi Rafsanjani but he was out of the country. Andrews spoke about the favourable welcome: 'They were thrilled at the idea that we would come to see them and they were generally overjoyed that we were there and that we had an open mind.'

At every available opportunity, the delegation pushed Keenan's Irish nationality and said that he would not get mixed up in politics. They received a clear indication that he was alive and that every effort would be made to have him released. Indeed, the delegation was told to expect some good news in the near future. But there were also indications that Iran was having difficulties with its contacts in Beirut, particularly after the release of Frank Reed and Robert Polhill, the Professor of Business Studies and Accounting at Beirut University College. The two Americans had been released with the help of Iran, and a lack of reciprocal action by the United States had weakened Teheran's links with the hostage-taking groups. The delegation also thought that the Iranians knew more about Keenan than they were saying. At the sisters' request, the politicians carried a message to the Iranians. They said that Brenda and Elaine wished to meet the families of the Iranian hostages as soon as possible. It was something the women had wanted for some time: 'We had met the families of most of the other hostages. These people were suffering every bit as much as we were and we had to meet them to let them know that and to give them support. It was what we wanted for a long time.' Elaine said that in some ways it was worse for the Iranians because there had been consistent reports that their hostages 'were living under so many death threats. You need death to be final – to see a body – to come back to normality, and these people were not given anything to prove that.'

On their return to Ireland, the delegation said that the release of hostages would be speeded up if there were increased efforts by the Americans to use their influence to encourage the release of the Iranian hostages being held in Lebanon. The sisters met the delegation in Dublin and were very happy with what they heard. 'The politicians gave the Iranians what they wanted – the chance to talk. The Iranians wanted communication. They did not really want to talk to us, although we were willing to go. They wanted to talk to higher-up people, people with power, and it happened.'

On 21 June, an earthquake in northern Iran killed 35,000 people and injured thousands more. The Irish government immediately sent £100,000 to the disaster fund. Britain, in comparison, the sisters say, was 'slow on the uptake'. Brenda rang Conor Murphy as soon as she heard about the earthquake and a telemessage with a note of condolence from the Keenan family was sent to the Iranian ambassador. 'You think about all the disasters in the world and everyone suffering and Iran is no different. It was ordinary people – farmers, down-to-earth people.' Elaine added: 'We knew nothing about Iran and when Brian was kidnapped, we got to know so much about the country. You had the gut feeling about the earthquake and it hadn't anything to do with Brian being kidnapped. You knew that the Western world was against them so much and you thought about who was going to give aid. Foreign Affairs now say that they ensured that their sending of aid was quick off the mark.' One official said, 'It was a gesture which was loud and clear.'

Sometimes the sisters met with criticism when they talked about helping Iran because many people in the North seemed to think that the Iranians were all terrorists. 'They would say that you were feeding those who took from you and we would always say that it was not like that. It's like being from Northern

Ireland. When you leave the country, you are classed as a terrorist whether you are or you aren't.' The women could not even condemn the kidnappers. 'They were given an order and they had to do something to feed their families.'

Shortly after the earthquake, Brenda and Frank McCallan met the Iranian ambassador in Dublin. Bahram Ghassemi told them that he was very pleased with the generous response of the Irish government and people. 'He said that they were a very caring people. He told us that he was doing all he could for Brian,' Brenda said, 'and he told me that he was speaking to me as he would to the sisters of the Iranian hostages. You classed that as a compliment.' The ambassador said that sometimes when he had seen the sisters on television, he had cried. Both women built up a very good relationship with Ghassemi. Later that year, he invited them to his leaving party. He told them not to blame every Iranian for what had happened to their brother. The sisters believe that they built up a good friendship with the Iranians because they were down-to-earth. 'We were nobodies. We had nothing for two years of the four and a half and we had to fight tooth and nail to get any information.'

At the beginning of July, Mick's diary entry says that Dr Eames had told them that Brian's release was imminent and that he would be coming out through Damascus. Noel O'Byrne, the chargé d'affaires in Iran, said that he could see the release happening in months and not days. He also gave them the startling news that, in Teheran, Brian had been known as Irish for only six months. This has never been confirmed, but the sisters believe that the media, particularly the British tabloids, have a lot to answer for because of their consistent portrayal of their brother as British: 'It was unbelievable. It mightn't have been that way in everyone else's eyes, but certainly for the family it was. You would only be out of the TV studio where you were asking them to call him Irish and they would be calling him a Briton again. We used to think that if a deal was struck with Britain, they would have thrown him out with the other hostages to get him off their hands.'

A few weeks earlier, the campaign group had held a day-long meeting to review its four years' work. Much of their time was taken up discussing the past campaign. Joe Lenaghan presented a paper on the future of the group. They had agreed to step up their campaign and had considered appointing an administrator to work from an office in Belfast. At this stage, they were resigned to the fact that Brian's release would take at least another year.

7

THE ROAD TO DAMASCUS

Brenda Gillham was sitting in her front room one evening at the beginning of July 1990. She and Elaine had just returned from Galway where a schoolfriend of Brian's, Gerald Dawe, had read his poem about their brother's kidnapping. In it, Dawe recalls the university days he and Keenan had spent in Coleraine:

> the seedy flats and houses, the booze,
> even those tweedy women still promenading,
> their silky scarves and solid shoes –
> a few sit beside me discussing stuffed courgettes
> while country music in the background
> wails its covert sexuality.

The poem had been the latest in a long line of events organised to keep the campaign alive. Suddenly, Brenda heard a car drawing to a halt outside her house. A carload of men shouted out: 'Fuck Brian Keenan. Free Michael Stone.' Stone is a loyalist extremist serving a life sentence for murdering six people, including three men at the funeral of the Gibraltar Three in Milltown cemetery on 16 March 1988. In some circles, he is regarded as a hero. After the incident, Brenda spoke to her neighbours. One said that her little girl had heard the remarks and was terrified. Brenda Gillham could do without this sectarian bullying. She was afraid.

On the drive back to Belfast earlier that day, Elaine had phoned her mother, who told her that reporters were looking for them.

Word was coming through the official Iranian news agency, IRNA, that the release was imminent. 'You needn't get yourselves settled down because it looks as if you're going to have to fly to Damascus,' Mrs Keenan said. When they reached Ballybeen, there were several reporters outside Brenda's home, so both women escaped to their mother's to plan what to do. As always, their mother was saying little: she never had allowed her hopes to be built up. Because of the bitter disappointment and sense of letdown they had felt in Dublin in January 1989, the sisters decided to stay put in Belfast. They remained more sceptical than optimistic about the report. This time, however, they thought that the source of the information offered them a glimmer of hope. The news agency was not inclined to publish spurious reports. Quoting informed sources in Beirut, IRNA had said that if a hostage was to be released, it would probably be Keenan. In the past, the Syrians, at military and diplomatic level, unofficially had played a key role in the mechanics of hostage releases. Two days later, a known hostage group contacted Syrian forces in Beirut to arrange for a hostage release.

Brenda and Elaine decided to keep the reporters and camera crews at bay. On previous occasions, particularly during and after Frank Reed's release, their doors had been open to the reporters and photographers. They made and received phone calls while they were being filmed by television cameras. Because of the lack of privacy, their children were becoming very unsettled.

Significantly, the Department of Foreign Affairs had received no official notification about a release. The sisters decided to stay in their own homes close by the phones. News reporters and camera crews were on standby for more than a week a few yards from Brenda's door. A satellite dish was also erected near the house. Many believed that the irony of ironies would happen – Brian Keenan would be released on the Twelfth of July. And it was to be no ordinary Twelfth because it was the tercentenary of the battle of the Boyne. Loyalist marches and demonstrations were bigger and more frequent than in other years. Unionist leaders at the best of times felt uncomfortable about Keenan, the Irish passport-holding Northern Protestant. A Twelfth release would have inspired little enthusiasm from them. The presence of camera crews and journalists in the loyalist Ballybeen estate, combined with the public preoccupation with Brian Keenan's passport, fuelled tension in the neighbourhood.

During the week of the Twelfth, Brenda's two youngest children, eleven-year-old Cheryl and nine-year-old Janeen, were sitting on the small grass slope facing their home. A white van went past and, out of its window, someone shouted 'Fenian lovers' within earshot of the youngsters. They ran in to their mother, asking her whether they were Protestants or Catholics. This was the final straw for Brenda; she was at breaking point. 'This was when it really hurt. They did not hear it in their own home and it had to come from strangers. Cheryl asked me did Catholics believe in God. I told her that they just have a different way of praying. At least you were able to explain it. That was the first time that my children ever asked me anything like that.'

In the early hours of the morning of 12 July, a petrol bomb was thrown onto the grass opposite the Gillham house, scorching a car belonging to a television crew. There was little reporting of the incident afterwards, despite the fact that many Belfast journalists covering the story knew what had happened. The media in general respected the sisters' wishes to play down the attack. Brenda Gillham now deliberately makes light of the incident, but she admits that it was alarming: 'You would have found those bottles lying about the estate. Seemingly that was a very rough night in the area. It was frightening; I was terrified.' She tried to keep the news away from the children, but they heard it reported on television.

The pressure on the families was intolerable. They considered moving to Dublin. Elaine was so angry, she decided to take the issue further: 'I went to try and find leading loyalists in the estate. I got no satisfaction there and I went to the local UDA [Ulster Defence Association] headquarters with Frank McCallan. I specifically wanted to find out if the incident was directed at Brenda's home and who carried it out. My first reaction was that my questions were falling on deaf ears and that these people did not want to know. We asked to speak with another man and someone else was brought in. We told him that we had kids in the home and that was where our concern lay.' The UDA told her that they would make sure that there would be no more trouble. They reassured Elaine that they had not instigated the attack. The meeting was nerve-wracking. 'We knew what was building up. We were still worried and you always got someone drunk coming up and saying something to you. Sometimes it was better to keep our mouths shut. It was our problem.' They tried to keep the incident away from their mother, but she read about it in the papers. Mick and Stephen and the children moved into a hotel, but the women were determined to stay in their own homes. 'If the word did break that he was getting out, we would be sitting inside, with the media outside. There was no way that we could have got out through the front door. The media were really going to inundate us and the kids would be screaming and crying and would be upset. That's why they moved quickly.'

Just as on several occasions in the past, speculation about an imminent release started to wane. National television crews and reporters started to leave the Ballybeen estate. 'It all went dead,' Brenda said. 'I must admit that when the reporters started to be called away, they were as sorry as we were. It was just like having a death in the family and, after the body is buried, you're on your own. When they were outside the house, we carried on as best as we could, but it was difficult. The BBC, ITN and Sky were there all the time. You tried to just go about your normal work. In the mornings, we would go out and give them a cup of tea, but they were always being followed.' 'You always watched behind your back because the reporters were following you,' Elaine said. 'When you went to the bank, they were certainly after you. When we went to get Trust money in the bank, we had to ring the bank manager to say we were coming down. He even had to come to the house once.'

In Dublin, members of the campaign group were attending a meeting with politicians who were interested in the Keenan case. As the news was beginning to die about an imminent release, the group decided to go and see Conor Murphy, from the consular section of Foreign Affairs. It is almost certain that Israeli bombing raids against Hezbollah positions in southern Lebanon had set back the release. The bombing had taken place close to residential areas. Joe Lenaghan remembers the meeting with senior officials: 'We could see that they were seriously embarrassed that something had gone wrong, but they would not say what it was. They told us confidentially that something had been about to happen and that there had been a setback.'

The campaign group called on the Irish government to issue an immediate statement condemning the Israelis for their actions. They did so. A few days later, Foreign Affairs told the campaign group members that something would happen within six weeks.

The officials were right. When the word finally came, Brenda and Elaine could not believe it. Reports started to filter through on the morning of 23 August. Elaine Spence received a phone call from a well-known radio journalist in the North, Eamonn Mallie. 'Eamonn rang up at 8.30 in the morning and said, "Sorry to ring you, Elaine, but it has all started up again." ' Elaine went straight to Brenda's house, a few minutes away. The source of information again was the Iranian news agency. 'We thought that IRNA could not make the same mistake twice.'

This time, however, they also got a phone call from Foreign Affairs, telling them to expect a call from the Taoiseach. 'Charles Haughey would not ring you for the fun of it,' Elaine said. 'Because our phones were constantly engaged, we had planned to get Charlie Haughey to ring on another phone.' Elaine left and told the reporters that she was going to work. 'You had to tell them always where you were going every time,' Brenda said. 'He had Elaine's work number and the women in the centre were warned not to answer the phone because Charlie was supposed to be ringing her.' Haughey did not ring Elaine at the women's centre; instead, he telephoned a neighbour of Brenda's, whose number the sisters had passed on to the Irish government a year before. 'When I got over, it was Charlie Haughey and he asked was it Brenda or Elaine. He did not mention anything about how they were waiting for the Syrians. All he said was that it was on. I was bursting at the seams.' They asked other group members to phone Foreign Affairs to try and get more information. They wanted to make sure that what they had been told was not a figment of their imagination. Brenda said Haughey had sounded very excited on the phone.

With Frank McCallan, the sisters decided to leave for Dublin the following morning. They had to dodge the media, who again had taken up camp in Ballybeen. 'We had it planned that Frank would come to my house,' Elaine said, 'pick up the clothes and put them in the boot. We were saying that it could still go wrong. We didn't get too built up.' Even Minnie Keenan seemed to be more hopeful: 'Before we left, my mother always said that she would never believe it until Brian was sitting in front of her. That morning, we rang her and she said he was coming home this time.' Their car was followed to Dublin by television crews. Close to Drogheda, one of the cars containing the BBC reporter, Noreen Erskine, flashed its lights. Brenda and Elaine's car stopped and Noreen told them that she had just been bleeped by Brenda's husband. When Brenda rang Mick, he told her that there was an announcement about the handover of a hostage. The handover time came and went. Brenda brought her knitting with her to Dublin. Before she left, her family had held a meeting. She tried to explain to her children why she was going to Dublin. 'If it had happened when we were in Belfast, we would have been torn between our brother and the children. I never worried about the children because I knew that they were all right with Mick.'

On the afternoon of 24 August, they had lunch with officials in Foreign Affairs. The mood was fairly jubilant. They went back to Buswells Hotel and were joking and laughing with the reporters who had gathered there. 'On other occasions when Brian was supposed to be released, you were locked up in your room and you never got eating, but this time it was very relaxed.'

That evening, Gerard Collins came to the hotel. 'At 6.45 we caught the news which said that the handover time had passed four hours. We thought, shit, this is definitely it. We thought this was the wind-down to a failure again,' Brenda said. But for once, their fears were not confirmed. Elaine and McCallan went to the door of Buswells to meet Collins. The steps and street were crowded with cameramen and journalists. Elaine presumed that the cameras were there to film Gerard Collins entering the hotel, but suddenly the cameras were filming her. ITN's Andy Simmons came forward and told her that Brian had been handed over. By this stage, Collins had got lost among the cameras. He came forward as Andy Simmons was telling her the news. 'Gerry Collins just stood and shook his head. I knew he wasn't saying to me that it wasn't going to happen, but he was saying hold on. They asked me to say something on TV and there was no way I could have. I looked at Frank McCallan and he put his thumb up and said, "We've done it", and I just burst out crying.'

The news had broken. They were then taken into the lift with Collins. 'Gerry came to our room and sat on a chair beside the bed. We flushed the toilet and ran the bath and shower because there was a journalist in the next room.' Collins brought them for a meal in the hotel and said that he was still concerned because there was no word coming through from the Syrians. 'We cut through the kitchens to where there was a room set up and you were wondering why that was going on, why that room had been set up. You always stopped eating when he was talking on the phone. It was the fifth phone call; that was the important one.' It came from Conor Murphy, who was phoning from Iveagh House. Foreign Affairs was reluctant to make any move to fly out to Damascus until definite word had come through. Shortly before, Daouk rang Murphy from Beirut to say that Keenan had been handed over to the Syrians. When Collins got the news, he spoke about flying out that night. Brenda baulked at the idea because there was a severe storm blowing and she was afraid to fly.

After getting the news, Collins calmly tucked into a steak. 'He said his information was from a reliable source. He said it was on and everyone at the table was looking at him as he finished his T-bone steak. We were all sitting ready to throw up over the dinner because we were so nervous,' Elaine said. When he had polished off his dinner, he turned to the sisters and said: 'Let's go out and face these vultures.' Collins announced he was happy to impart the good news that Brian Keenan had been released. The sisters knew then that the release was definite and they went with Collins into the lobby of the hotel to speak to the media. He had a press statement ready.

At three in the morning, the sisters took baths and hoped to get a few hours' sleep. They turned on the television in their room, wanting to see pictures of the handover. 'We really needed to see him being handed over because we did not know how bad he was going to look and what our reactions were going to be. For years reporters had said to us, "What will you say to him?" But it wasn't a case of that, it was more his expression. We were trying to get ourselves prepared for not looking shocked for his sake.' They left their hotel for the airport at 5 am, travelling there in a government limousine. On the way out, reporters shook their hands and wished them good luck. Elaine remembers thinking about the following twenty-four hours and says that she and her sister were terrified. 'Fear really hit us for the first time. We were thinking about all the things which had happened in the four and a half years.'

Earlier, there had been some debate about who would fly to Damascus on the Irish government's jet. It had been agreed that Frank McCallan would travel with the sisters to Damascus. Joe Lenaghan counted up the number of seats on the plane and the number of people scheduled to travel on it. He remembers quizzing Foreign Affairs about an extra seat which was vacant when the plane left Dublin. They were also curious about why the aircraft had to stop in Rome. 'They tried to disguise it by saying that they had to stop to refuel. When they spoke about the person they were going to pick up in Rome, they were always very vague about who he was.' Some have speculated that the man picked up in Rome may have been a negotiator in a deal for Keenan's release, but Foreign Affairs said that it was Padraig Murphy, the head of the department's political division. The campaign group had planned that all its members would have a role to play when Brian was released. While Brenda, Elaine and Frank flew to Damascus, Joe Lenaghan made arrangements for everyone who was arriving in Dublin; Terri Hooley came to Brenda's home in Ballybeen to answer the phone.

On their way to the airport, the government limousine was stopped for speeding, but it was soon waved on when an explanation was given to the Gardaí. 'When we got to the airport, people were clapping and cheering. We went into a small room where there was a man and a woman and we sat across from them. The woman was called Bridget and she introduced herself as the nurse. She said, "Thank God this has happened." She said she did not think that she could have taken another time because she was always on standby at other times when the

Government thought that Brian was going to be released. The man with her was the doctor.'

The sisters were still fearful of a last-minute hitch: 'Deep down in your heart, you still thought on the flight that something could still go wrong. It was hard enough the four times he was meant to get out, but to sit in Damascus and be rejected, that would have been too hard.' The flight lasted more than six hours. Gerard Collins sat with officials from his department at the front of the plane. The doctor and nurse stayed with Brenda, Elaine and Frank. The journey over was fairly relaxed and they spent most of their time reading newspapers. They left the jet for half an hour when they arrived in Rome to pick up Padraig Murphy. The plane seemed to have landed some distance from the main runway. They had tea and coffee in a room at the airport. Later, when they were back in the jet, the pressure proved too much for Frank McCallan: 'Brenda and I were sitting opposite each other reading the news and Frank was listening to music on his personal stereo and I noticed that he was crying. His face was getting redder and redder and it wasn't like Frank. What could you say? The tears were tripping him and I reached over and squeezed his knee, saying it was over.'

The arrival in Damascus on 25 August at 1.30 pm was an intimidating experience. 'It was a different matter when you landed there. All those tears that you wanted to shed just weren't there. There was no way you could have cried. The two of us travelled in tracksuits, thinking that we would not offend anyone in this foreign country and the next thing was, as soon as the door opened, you felt the heat. You breathed in and nothing came in at all.' Before they left the plane, Collins showed them a schedule of events which would include twenty minutes alone with Brian.

They were taken into the airport lounge and were brought orange juice. Trying to talk about anything other than Brian's release, the sisters ended up discussing the decor of the airport. 'All of a sudden a Syrian TV crew came along and pounced on us, and all we could say was that we wanted to thank everyone. We could hardly speak.' They were seated on a settee with Frank McCallan while Collins and various diplomats stood talking at the other end of the room. McCallan wanted to steal a saucer with the name of Damascus airport on it. 'Brenda and Elaine wouldn't let me take it. They both grabbed me by the arms and said that I might get my hands cut off if I took it.'

Brenda was terrified about meeting Brian. 'I always had it in my mind that he would be a lot thinner and that he might see the shock in our faces. I did not know what to say first to him.' The sisters were also scared that Brian's beard would be shaved off by his captors. In the airport lounge, they were surrounded by Syrians. 'We sat facing a line of Syrians sitting on a settee and their eyes never left us. If you looked straight ahead, you had to be looking at them and your eyes were wandering everywhere. Frank was very calm then,' said Elaine. The sisters were conscious that the place was dominated by men. They also felt powerless because there was nothing practical that they could do but wait. Collins then told them that they would have to go to the Dutch embassy where they would be phoned.

They were there for more than two hours. Elaine says that when they were given the definite handover time, she felt very empty. 'I wanted to cry, but it was not there. I felt enclosed because we were bundled from a car to a car to a building. The Syrian media was there too and that was hard to cope with. I just felt like a shell – completely empty.' Brenda was frightened and could not take it all in. 'I had a fear of meeting Brian from the night before in Dublin. I was afraid that he would not recognise us.'

The party left the Dutch embassy shortly before 4 pm and travelled to the Syrian foreign office. Elaine said: 'You still didn't honestly believe that this was it. On the road to Damascus, Gerard Collins said this was the road where God saw the light and Brenda corrected him and said it was Saint Paul. In Damascus the streets were empty and gunmen were every fifty yards along the route. Even the kids had Kalashnikovs.' For a short while, the women thought that they were en route to Beirut. Suddenly, the car swerved right. 'We saw loads of media and those big wrought-iron gates, and it was like we were home. We'd seen so many hostages walking down those steps and it was never ours,' Brenda said. Inside the Syrian foreign office, they were brought into a large room; a photograph of President Assad was on a wall. They were still fearful that something was going to go wrong because everything had happened so quickly. 'We had no sooner arrived into the room than someone said, "Mr Brian, all stand".'

They had never heard their brother being called that before. Brian Keenan did not know that he was going to meet his sisters and Frank McCallan in that room: 'I thought that I could have been going to see Syrian intelligence for another session.' Brian had been kept in the building for three days and two nights, ignorant of when anyone was going to come and get him. He had been under heavily armed guard everywhere he went; he had even been followed into the shower. Through English-language newspapers he had read about the speculation concerning his release.

He walked into the room, surrounded by about half a dozen Syrians, clutching a carrier bag to his chest. 'When he walked into the room,' Elaine said, 'neither of us knew what to do. My first impression was that he had shrunk. I ran over to him and said, "You haven't changed." ' When he saw his sisters, he stood still and threw his hands above his head saying 'Oh Christ'.

Keenan thought they should have been given some time alone. Ten months after his release, he described his first impressions of seeing his sisters: 'When I walked in, I saw them standing there looking so puzzled and there were also these dignitaries whom I did not know. It was the riveting of every eye in that room on me. I just saw so many eyes looking at me. They were all wondering who is this thing. It was like frozen human beings looking intensely. It was like coming out of the womb. What would you say if you could speak?'

Brenda said that she could not take the first step to meet him: 'I don't know why...We were surrounded by men whom we did not know and I did not know what to do. Should I go forward or not? I was always aware of the difference in culture.' Brian told Elaine to stop crying and asked how they had got there so quickly. Keenan believes that the women were feeling a mixture of confusion and relief, but there were also big question marks. Elaine recalls: 'I thought he was going to pull out all my hair. He said he had to go back to Beirut because all his things were there and he kept repeating himself.' He was adamant that he did not want the nurse or doctor. 'He kept throwing his hands up. The nurse came over to him and he said that she was the first woman he had met in a long time. A few minutes before, he said he did not want her anywhere near him,' Elaine said.

As soon as he put his arms around them, his sisters felt his strength. The doctor gave him dark glasses to wear. 'His eyes were very protruding. You could see the horror in his face.'

As they were leaving Syrian foreign affairs, someone came out after him, saying, 'Brian, your souvenirs'. It was the bag containing his clothes and newspapers. En route to the Dutch embassy, he asked about the American hostages, Lieutenant Colonel William Higgins and the British lecturer, Leigh Douglas, and they told him that they had been killed. When they arrived at the Dutch embassy, the first thing he tried to do was telephone his mother in Belfast. He could not get a line.

Both Frank McCallan and the sisters say that the two hours in the Dutch embassy were very tense. Brian spoke on the phone to Charles Haughey. Collins jokingly told him that his drinking would be restricted to Guinness on the flight home. The release had happened very quickly. The sisters now say that they were given little or no assistance from Foreign Affairs about what to expect after the release. 'We were handed bits of paper on the flight. We didn't know what was ahead of us either.'

Brian asked them what they had been doing in his absence. 'We told him about the French hostage, Sontag, and how he provided the first evidence that he was alive. We told him about going to see Frank Reed and he replied by saying that while he was sitting chained in his cell, his sisters were flying all around the world having a big holiday.' In the Dutch embassy, an official from Foreign Affairs was typing up a press release. The sisters became preoccupied with what Brian was going to eat. They watched him take two bowls of cold soup.

Brian agrees that there was a lot of tension in the room in the Dutch embassy. He says that Collins was very concerned about what he was going to say. 'You felt like an alien from outer space. After four and a half years, you come out with really very heightened awareness. I could feel the eyes of the doctor and the nurse watching me all the time. After four and a half years, you could pick out every emotion of everybody in that room.' He recalls trying to crack jokes to break the ice. 'All I wanted was a piece of chocolate cake, an Irish coffee and some ice cream.'

The three had little time to talk alone. When he said that he had to tell Mr and Mrs McCarthy that John was all right, they told him the sad news. He broke down when he heard about Sheila's death. 'We were so scared to tell him that,' Brenda said. 'He broke in a very sweet personal way, not in floods of tears. To me, I might as well have said that our mother was dead and he would have reacted in the same way.' Brian agrees.

When Collins showed him the typed press release, Brian wanted some of it changed and deleted what he did not like. 'His sharpness showed right away. When he said that he was going to go back to Beirut, we thought, Oh Christ, you can't argue with this man. He had a mind of his own,' Elaine said. Cameras were clicking in the room. Keenan covered his eyes and asked who was taking the photographs.

He talked a lot about the men he had left behind. 'He knew what he wanted to say about the other hostages. He said he had to get something to each of the families that they would recognise and know them by.' On the plane home, Frank McCallan told him about a lot of the other bad news, like the death of their friend Buzz Logan. 'We were scared about what his reaction was going to be. You're in a plane and it's so enclosed and it wasn't a place for anyone to bring all their emotions out or to turn angry or anything. What was going to hurt him was going to hurt us.' Brenda said she wanted to tell him in just a few hours everything that had happened in the four and a half years. But she remembered Frank Reed's words: 'Don't rush it.'

On the flight home, Keenan was desperately trying to read articles on events about which he knew nothing. He was quiet for most of the flight: 'I could see the doctor and the nurse still staring at me. I deliberately wanted to take everything, everything, in. Papers. News. I totally submerged my mind in information that I knew nothing about. I'm an awfully emotional man, but I wasn't going to perform for anyone. I kept asking, What's the story behind this and that? I just wanted to pile everything in to keep the mind working above the heart. It was the only way that I could hold myself together.'

Brenda did not expect her brother to show any emotion. The sisters realised within minutes of meeting him that they had got the old Brian back – 'still the strong stubborn git that he had always been'.

When he talked on the plane about the ending of the Iran–Iraq war, they were relieved because they knew that there had not been a mental block during his captivity. The sisters both thought that Brian had acquired a bit of an English accent. He told them that he and the other hostages had been given books and magazines like *Time* and *Newsweek*, often with certain pages torn out. They were worried in case he was going to argue with the officials and Gerard Collins on the flight back. He told them that he had been let out of captivity dressed like a 'fucking clown' by his captors. When he was first released he was wearing size 44 trousers and a pair of orange and blue moccasins. Later the Syrians gave him a grey cotton suit.

He went to the back of the jet for a short sleep. Collins asked him if he needed a pillow and Brian refused. Collins lifted his head and put the pillow under it. Brian asked for the lights to be put out. He was lying flat on his back at one point and the top half of his body jumped up. He shouted, 'Toilet! Toilet!' and his eyes were really protruding. He then lay back down again. 'He was really like a corpse then. He had needed to lie down to compose himself and to take in some of the things he had been told.'

His sisters felt very possessive of him: 'We wanted to share him, but we did not want to let go. You were afraid to let go. After what you had gone through, you were afraid to let go in case something happened.' On the plane, they were able to mull over the last four and a half years. Brenda thought that Brian's return was like someone coming back from the dead and also like someone being born: 'It seemed as if a lifetime went by since we last saw him until he got out. There was the emotion of him giving us hugs, which he did not do before. That was strange. Trying to talk to him was like a baby beginning to talk and for you to find your feet it was like a baby beginning to walk. That's the only way that I can describe it.' During the journey, a Foreign Affairs official asked Keenan if he would do a press conference, but he refused.

Still thinking that Brian was not going to give the press conference, the sisters had arranged that Brenda would bring him to the Mater private hospital while Elaine conducted the meeting. 'We told him to change into his normal clothes and you could see that he could not be annoyed. Then he did and you could see that he was full of muscle. We were trying to make him look better than he did,' Brenda said. Towards the end of the journey, he sat cross-legged in the plane and they asked him to sign the visitors' book. He said that he did not know if he could write. 'You could see him looking out the porthole windows and he was like a mad man.' Some of the officials started singing 'Molly Malone' when they saw the first lights of Dublin. Elaine remembers looking at her brother and seeing complete fear in his eyes: 'He just stared and stared and then he started to rock and, all of a sudden, we had landed.' On 25 August at 11.12 pm, Brian Keenan had arrived back in Ireland.

Standing at the top of the steps of the plane, Brian hesitated when he saw all the people at the airport, many of whom were banging on windows. The sisters panicked because Collins had told them a short time earlier that a small group of family and friends would be waiting to greet them. At the bottom of the steps, Keenan met Charles Haughey and Pat O'Connor. When Keenan walked along the red carpet, he moved off it for a while because he was following the sound of the people beating on the windows. Brenda recalls feeling very proud: 'You never thought so many people cared so much.'

Once inside the airport, they were brought in to meet politicians and church leaders. Dr Eames was among those who had gathered: 'For one awful moment, I remember thinking this cannot be Brian Keenan. I was so moved that I could hardly speak.' A few minutes later, Brian went into the VIP lounge where his family and friends were. There were approximately thirty adults and twenty children there.

Jim McIlwaine remembers: 'We were watching it on the television and then he arrived into the room. It all became one.' The sisters could hear children screaming and people shouting before they entered the room. They had planned to get in there before Brian to tell everyone to keep the noise down and approach him slowly, but it did not happen that way. He did not recognise some of his friends. With hindsight, they think that fewer people should have been there to meet him.

Elaine remembers: 'As soon as I walked in there, I saw Stephen and the tears were rolling down his cheeks and we could not speak to each other. I could not tell you who was in that room. All of a sudden Brian was out of the room and we were saying, "Where is Brian? Who went with him?"' Keenan had been taken in to meet Frank Reed.

Then, suddenly, he was doing the press conference. 'That was always Brian. Quick on decisions,' Elaine said. It had been agreed earlier that Elaine would read out Brian's statement. They said that the only time he was nervous during the press conference was when he talked about John McCarthy. He spoke for about ten minutes. Elaine believes that Brian had planned what he was going to say. He said later that he had made notes on the plane. They were anxious that he should say something for their mother before he left the press conference. When a journalist chirped in that there was a woman waiting, Brian told him that he did not want to talk to him. It transpired that the journalist was trying to get Keenan to pass on a message to his mother.

Before the press conference, Charles Haughey had told them that it was the family's night and that he did not wish to be in front of the cameras. 'He had to be actually coaxed to come onto the stage. As soon as he had said his bit, he left. You could see that he did not want to make a stand out of it because he knew what damage could be done,' Elaine said.

The sisters were alarmed when Brian was taken away from them. 'I think that it all happened very quickly,' Elaine said. 'People think that you should go back to normality very quickly.'

The sisters think now that it would have been a good idea for them to have spent a few days in Damascus alone with their brother. At that very early stage, they wanted to be the family they had never been before.

8

UNDER THE SPOTLIGHT

That night, Elaine Spence could not sleep. She sat up for hours in her bedroom in the Skylon Hotel, minutes from the Mater private hospital where Brian was recuperating. Stephen and her nine-year-old daughter, Ashleigh, lay sleeping, but she could not settle. Earlier that evening, she had had a silly row with Brenda about the carrier bag that Brian was holding when they had first seen him in Damascus. Brian had given it to Brenda to look after. Elaine wanted to read the newspapers which were inside, but Brenda would not allow her to. Elaine was still thriving on press reports about the release.

Things were far from perfect between Elaine and Stephen. They had gone back to their hotel after the press conference. Stephen told Elaine to talk away about the trip to Damascus, saying that he wanted to hear all about it. 'He was telling me not to worry, that he would stay awake and he told me to get it all off my chest. At that time, it was the last thing that I wanted to do.' Ashleigh was also in the room and she was extremely excited. 'Stephen knew that it was a hopeless case for us to talk openly at that time. Everyone settled down for the night and I just sat in the dark. I had taken too much in my head. Stephen had thought that the best way would be for me to sit up talking, which would have been me before, but not then. My brain was so confused. I was not ready to talk. I certainly was not ready to

131

sit down and explain to him what it was like. I kept telling him to keep quiet.' Elaine now realises that Stephen was trying to comfort her.

A few doors away, Brenda and Mick were also having problems. Mick was trying to coax his wife into eating some food. Both women had been on the go since five o'clock the previous morning and it was now well past midnight. Their children, who were sleeping in another room, were eager to talk, but Brenda could not. She left the room, slamming the door. She wanted to go for a walk. 'Mick got angry and told me that I was not going out because it was a strange place and I told him not to stop me. I told my oldest girl, Joanne, to get the children out of my sight, and that was very hurtful.' Brenda found the hotel claustrophobic. 'When I got back, I felt that I was closed in Brian's cell. He had left it and I was still in it.'

The next morning, both women were wondering where the rest of the campaign group were. It was the first thing that Elaine said to Stephen when he awoke. She now says that by making a remark like that, she was rejecting him. 'He told me that he could not sit back and see other men rule my life. He felt helpless because he thought that he was doing nothing; I felt so helpless because he could see other men telling me what to do and what not to do and he was not being brought into the conversation.' Both women realised then how dependent they had become on the other members of the group: 'We were in a different world. You needed the group, you thrived on it. We sapped the life out of Joe, Jim and Frank, trying to find out what was going on. We were so used to working around these men. Our men were never there because they were always left minding the children.' Elaine said that it was only when Stephen lost his temper that morning that she began to realise what an important part he had played in the whole thing.

Brian Keenan talks about how, after his release, he and his sisters were placed under the spotlight of the world: 'What was thrown together was the image that the media had of us and we had to respond to it at the press conference.' That Sunday morning, 26 August, the sisters went to visit Brian in hospital. 'That was when Brian told us about the fears he had for us. He knew that we could have got a lot of stick about the Irish passport because of where we lived and that it could endanger us quite a bit. Brian said that he feared for our lives because of the passport and he knew that we were not the favourites among some people in the North because of the passport.'

The sisters reassured him that they had not been given much bother and were fit to cope with anything that happened. Elaine remembers that it was strange to visit Brian in hospital. 'It was like going to see anyone in hospital. We were still in shock.' Ten months after the release, she would admit that, on some occasions, they considered classing Brian as British. 'At times when Brian was being classed as Irish, some journalists told us that they felt that it was safer to talk about him as British in some circumstances. We were torn, wondering were we right talking about him as Irish. You knew by people's reactions if it was silence or whatever because you were treading on dangerous ground. But turn the coin, and they would have done the same. There was concern from the Protestant people, but there just was not that wee touch of warmth from the Northern people.'

The sisters were scared to tell Brian too much because they

did not want an immediate reaction from him about what they had been doing during his captivity. They also say that Dr Eames had asked a psychiatrist to study tapes of other hostages after their release to see how they had reacted. The sisters told Brian about their travels to various countries to try and seek his release. 'He joked and said that we were darting around the world when he was in chains for four and a half years.' Brian Keenan spoke about the two things he had wanted for his family when he was being held captive. He wanted his sisters to do different things, to see the world and to get out of their routine; and he wished that his mother would be alive at the time of his release.

Four days after the release, Minnie Keenan paid her first visit to Dublin to visit her son in hospital. She saw him alone for several hours. Elaine remembers the change in her mother afterwards: 'She was a lot more content and a big weight seemed to have been lifted off her shoulders. She was much more relaxed and easy-going.'

Both sisters agree they wanted the family to become closer, despite their differences. They feel bitter that friends of Brian's who had not been involved in the campaign took over: 'We felt that people started appearing in Dublin who got a chance to spend more time with Brian than we did. We saw that Brian was a lot easier with friendship than family.' They saw very little of him while he was in hospital. 'All we wanted was the security of seeing him there. You needed that because it all happened so quickly. We knew that he was always a wanderer, but after four and a half years of being locked up and after what the families went through, all we wanted was two or three days with him.' Immediately after the release, they had spoken about how they had wanted to spend a few days alone with him. They now realise that if they had done that, they would all have gone insane.

A week afterwards, the women returned to Belfast with Frank McCallan. They were not looking forward to going back. They remember driving into Belfast with McCallan, agreeing that the place was dead of emotion. 'In my own way, I did not want to come back,' Brenda said. 'The heartache was so familiar there in the home and I thought that I would have had time to think about the time that I had lost with the children. How do you get that back?' Even things like helping their children with their homework had eluded the women during Brian's captivity. Mick, Brenda realised, had become both the father and the mother during that time.

Both women agree that Belfast was dead compared to Dublin where, they say, everyone was very affectionate: 'It was so good in Dublin because you managed to get through even to little children. We knew that we were coming back to a hostility in the North in which we had lived all our lives,' Elaine said. Even friends and people on the estate did not want to talk about the release. 'Very close friends knew that our minds were not our own. They could see that we were still in the land of limbo,' Brenda said. She recalls a man on the estate who used to keep clippings for her of anything that appeared about the hostage issue in the *Sunday Express*. He told her shortly after the release that he was looking forward to the party. It never happened.

While they were still in Dublin, a row was brewing about whether Belfast City Council should give Brian Keenan the freedom of the city. It was the last thing that they needed or wanted. The press officer of the Democratic Unionist Party,

Sammy Wilson, said on radio that one of the first things the sisters did was to contact Sinn Féin after the kidnap. 'That was a blatant lie,' Brenda said. Wilson and independent unionist councillor, Frank Millar, said that the council should have 'nothing to do' with Brian Keenan because he had taken out an Irish passport. Keenan watched Sammy Wilson on television in the Cock Tavern in Howth. He had slipped out of the hospital with a few friends for a drink. Later, at his Dublin Castle press conference, he would speak about how he had held a young baby in his arms in that bar. Wilson's inflammatory remarks were far from his mind.

The freemanship of Belfast was put forward by SDLP councillor, Dr Brian Feeney, without consulting the campaign group. The group rang him and told him to knock the proposal on the head. Feeney later said that he did not want to make a 'political football' out of the issue. Jackie Redpath, a community worker on the Shankill Road, went on radio and told the politicians and political parties to lay off Keenan. The family also was furious: 'The freedom of the city thing really annoyed us. How can you want the freedom of the city when it is in chains?'

Brian Keenan's return to Belfast was an opportunity for the city fathers to salvage some of their long-lost credibility. 'At that time, the world and his sister was watching Northern Ireland. Brian had been one bit of good news which came out of here and certain people let themselves down very badly. It wised me up so much to the bitterness. Did you ever hear anyone say once "What religion is John McCarthy?" ' The sisters had hoped that people would forget about politics and just be glad that their brother was home. Brenda says that Sammy Wilson did not have the guts to repeat his claims when Brian came back to Belfast, but this was no great surprise.

Elaine said: 'I became much more aware of society in Northern Ireland. You don't particularly like it but you have to accept it to a degree because of living here. Children are so expressive and up-to-date in Dublin. In Belfast, eleven-year-olds talk about food parcels and prison visits. Belfast has lost that human touch and it's a pity. There's definitely a coldness about the people here.' She said that her brother does not want any public recognition for what he went through. Keenan agrees, saying angrily: 'I don't want a rubber stamp from ignorant minds to tell me that I was a freeman of Belfast. I was a freeman long before them. Frank Millar and Sammy Wilson had a chance to make Belfast, all of it, festive and let what was instinctively there in the hearts and minds of all the people of the city be seen by the world's media, but instead these men chose to spit out venom, which in the end only demeaned them. That remains a profound insult to that quality of goodness and compassion which is instinctively in the nature of so many people that I have known for so long. Frank Millar and Sammy Wilson did not even go to the city hall because they knew that they could not win.'

When Brian Keenan returned to Belfast on 15 September, a large crowd turned out to greet him at Central Station. He travelled by train with his sisters and Frank McCallan. Both women initially panicked, thinking that Brian was going to go first to the west of the city rather than to his mother's house in east Belfast, but Brian left Central Station and went straight to Mayflower Street a few minutes away. Neighbours came out to greet him and he ran up the street, shaking their hands. Minnie

Keenan was very relaxed and posed for photographs with her son on the steps of her home.

On 17 September, they attended a reception in Belfast City Hall. The decision to hold a reception had been taken some time before by the lord mayor, Fred Cobain. Keenan had been a political pawn in Beirut. His return to Belfast did not change this situation, Brenda said: 'You knew that when the day came for his release, that it would be a case of going from the pot to the frying pan. The hassle about the reception was the last thing we needed. What else can you ask from your own people?' Before the lunch, Brian Keenan gave a short press conference. The conversation at the lunch, which was attended by city councillors and members of the campaign group, was very awkward. The sisters are disgusted that, afterwards, their brother was not even escorted out of the building, but was left at the top of the staircase by the lord mayor.

Meanwhile, people were gathering at the front of the city hall. The front gates had been closed. Keenan insisted that they be opened. He then met the people of Belfast.

There was a further furore when, two days later, Keenan shook hands with the Sinn Féin president, Gerry Adams, at a reception in Conway Mill, a former mill on the Falls Road which is used for local businesses, educational programmes, meetings and social functions. Sinn Féin had been approached by the campaign group and was warned not to make any mileage out of the homecoming. The reception had been organised by the Falls Community Council. A photograph of the handshake appeared in the *Irish News* the next day. Brenda said: 'I can understand him meeting the people, but the danger was him meeting Gerry Adams.' The sisters feared retaliation but Elaine remembers what Brian had told her on the plane on the way back from Damascus: 'He said that there would be nothing behind closed doors and that everything would be public. He said that he would shake hands with anyone.' His sisters had always maintained that there would be no party political involvement in the campaign to set him free: 'Within forty-eight hours of him being kidnapped, we decided that no party or organisation would be involved and we kept that up. I can see his point if he takes Gerry Adams as a man, but what we were wondering was where were his friends who were looking after him.'

Elaine dreaded telling Stephen about the incident: 'He did not know what we were all congregating for. He heard my conversation with Joe Lenaghan on the phone and I mentioned the words Gerry Adams. He was very cool, calm and collected, considering what my fears were.' Two days later, she was walking through the estate on her way to work. 'A kid cycled by me and spat at me. He had every right to spit at me if that was how he felt.' The effects of the Sinn Féin visit were also apparent in Brenda's home. She thought that it could cause her husband to walk out. Instead, he 'fell deathly quiet and that was worse than anything'.

Brenda told her brother shortly after the Gerry Adams incident that he should try to put himself into their situation. Brian believes that the photograph was a set-up and said that he was very relieved that there had been no subsequent retaliation. But the sisters were still concerned for their safety: 'You thought that if anything was going to happen, it would not happen right away. It was like sitting on eggs.' Nevertheless no one in their estate said anything about the handshake with Adams.

Later that week, Brian attended an event on the Shankill Road where he met the former lord mayor, Reg Empey, independent unionist Hugh Smyth, and other community workers and friends. The Shankill group asked that the event not be publicised, but the sisters decided that it would be prudent to take a photograph of him there and send it to the newspapers.

A month after his release, both women were beginning to feel like outsiders. They believe that Brian found it easier to go back to friendships rather than a relationship with his own family: 'I still think he has a struggle and that will last for a long time. It's very hard when Brian will not sit down and listen to you,' Elaine said. Through various chat shows, like 'The Late Late Show' on RTE and 'Kelly' on UTV, they learnt a lot about what he had endured during his captivity. 'When you are together, he will not talk about it,' Brenda said. 'Whether it's fear or not, I don't know. He just struck up a better relationship with his friends.'

But Brian Keenan himself does not see this as the whole picture: 'A mind and a personality needs to remake itself, slowly, searchingly, without external pressure from family friends or media demands. You've got to have some grasp of what you are before you know what you can give.' When the three went to Dublin to visit the families of the Iranian hostages in November 1990, Elaine says that Brian told her that he was going to shock everyone by asking to go back to Beirut. She told him that she was not surprised. He wanted the authority to go into Beirut and an assurance that he would be safe. He wanted to go back to secure the release of the other hostages. 'That was no shock because that was Brian,' Elaine said. Meeting the hostage families was very important for the women; they had been asking for it for several years. 'There's a bond between the families of hostages and we felt so sorry for them. For a long time, Brian was the forgotten hostage, but people never knew about the Iranians because of less publicity. We wanted to show them that we cared.'

Something else happened at this time. Before Keenan's kidnap, Elaine and Brenda said that their family was very undemonstrative. Since his release, they needed and wanted to touch him. Up until then, they had hugged and kissed, but in November the sisters noticed a change. 'We found that he needed to touch us – that showing of affection switched off very quickly. I remember the first cold point after meeting the Iranian hostage families. Brian said he was going to the bank and he shook hands with us and I thought, that's cold. That was a changing point,' Brenda said.

Brian's lack of communication made them feel rejected. 'I knew rejection when it came,' Brenda said. Elaine says that during her brother's captivity, she did not allow herself time to think about such an eventuality: 'You would not have had time in four and a half years to build yourself up for rejection. You would not have had the time to consider it.' She believes that professional counselling would have been a great help to them throughout Brian's captivity.

The sisters maintain that their brother does not want to become a hero. They also believe that Brian will never be able to live in Northern Ireland: 'If he lived here, he would always be made political. People in power in Northern Ireland know that he mixes with both sides of the community. That was Brian all his life and he can't switch off. The political hierarchy are now trying to use him and we think that is a bloody disgrace. Where were they in the last four and a half years?'

Early in 1991, Brian, Brenda and Elaine attended a dinner in

Stormont Castle, given by the Northern Ireland Office (NIO). One of the NIO ministers, Dr Brian Mawhinney, was there. Days after his release, while the sisters were still in Dublin, the NIO phoned one of their homes, inviting them to dinner. When they returned to Belfast, an NIO official met them to discuss the details. He told them not to publicise the dinner. A long list of prior commitments with family, friends and old associates caused Brian to put off the dinner. The open invitation lapsed for many months in the wake of the meeting with Adams. When the Brooke initiative – the Secretary of State's attempt to get inter-party talks going in the North – was announced, it was back on again. Before they entered the room where they would dine, Keenan asked one of his sisters to point out Dr Mawhinney. They also speak about how a senior official at the dinner table made a gaffe, saying that Brian Keenan had been away for ten years. 'People in the North are going to try and portray Brian as a peacemaker and they will try and use him,' Elaine said. 'At the end of the day, you lose faith and possibly your life. If Brian could only walk on one side, it would drive him insane.'

Shortly after the NIO dinner, Brenda recalls meeting a clergyman in Belfast who had spoken to his congregation about Elaine and herself. He described the sisters as being like the tale of the lost sheep: 'He spoke about the shepherd leaving the ninety-nine to look for the lost one. When he said it, it hit me like a bolt of lightning. We dropped everything for Brian and we didn't see it.'

Elaine remembers how she and Stephen argued about Brian's nationality: 'I had a different view of life from Stephen and I'm not saying that I'm right, but it all boiled down to the passport. It wasn't as big a shock to us. I remember saying to him not to ask me to decide between him and Brian.' After a few drinks on a Saturday night, they would argue about it. 'Stephen and I agree that we cannot remember good things in the years that Brian was held hostage. Stephen was asked a lot about Brian's Irish passport in work. I don't think that he ever got hassle, but you knew that when things were bad, there was silence.' Elaine's mind was on a different level during those years and she largely neglected her relationship with Stephen. But nobody, she says, could compete.

The sisters believe that the period also had a lasting effect on their children. 'Every time we went away, they said, "Where is Brian and why didn't you bring him home?"' When Elaine thinks of the saddest thing during those years, she does not, like Brenda, talk of Christmas. 'The saddest thing for me was watching pages turn yellow. The newspaper cuttings were going yellow and then brown and you were getting nowhere. That was hard to accept.'

Brenda wants to try to make up for lost time by taking a holiday with her children. Exactly a year after Brian's release, she managed to get away to Donegal for three days with her children. The entire experience has broadened her life. 'Before it all happened, my home was my nest. All of a sudden this happened and you realised what was going on, not only in the Middle East but also in your own country.' It forced her to think more about people outside her own community. 'The whole thing opened up an awful lot for me. I realised that human life was worth much more than religion. It has made me think more.' She has also become a stronger person. 'I would not let people walk on me any more. You only realise that when you become strong.' She has become much more politically informed and says she will stay that way. She is maddened when reporters ring up and say that it is Terry Waite's anniversary or that of someone else who is being held. 'There's no way that I will ever forget those dates because they are burnt into my mind. Just because Brian Keenan is out does not mean that we have forgotten.'

The sisters say that they have a lot to confide to their brother. 'All we want to say to him is that we have suffered as well. We never know where he is and if he could only ring or send a postcard, it would help. His friends know more than us and that is hard.' Before his kidnap, the family had little in common with him. They feel now that that has changed: 'We have things in common if we only had the chance to talk to him. It's awkward when people ask you about him. People don't believe that he is away all the time.' Elaine also believes that, to a degree, the media ruled their lives. 'If someone said to me that I was back to normality, I would be over the moon, but I don't think I know what normality is and you forget who you were,' Elaine said.

Readjusting their lives is proving to be very difficult. Both hate being known as Brian Keenan's sisters: 'I had my own identity before but I lost it and I'm trying to bring that back now. It's terribly hard to do. You need to have your own identity to pick up the pieces and get back to normality,' Elaine said. Neither woman feels that they are near the restoration of a normal life: 'I just wish he would class us as two human beings even more so than sisters. We might have a better relationship then,' Elaine said.

Brenda said: 'Maybe I put Brian before everybody else and that's the problem. I know that I was completely obsessed with him. I find that looking back to his release, I did not want to let him go. You lived in fear for four and a half years and it's very hard to forget that fear.'

Both their private and public lives are still affected: 'Once people, grateful as we are for their support, stop mentioning Brian Keenan to us in the streets, that will help us forget. We were up there in the limelight and we want to come back down again.' The women realise too that they have to leave one another's sides and get on with their own lives individually and no longer be the 'terrible twosome' that their brother often calls them.

9

A CHANCE TO TALK

Another concern, unexpected, but heavily insistent, is the effect
of our release on our families. Their process of withdrawal and
readjustment is a painful and confusing one and in many respects
mirrors my own . . . Much change has occurred in them as in me.
In the family circle a complicated and careful get-to-know-me
game is undertaken . . . My desire to protect them collides with
their understandable passion to possess a brother.

A section from Brian Keenan's address to the British Association of
Editors' lunch in London in March 1991

Ten months after Brian's release, the sisters read this speech and
seem to gain a better understanding of their brother's dilemma.
Sitting with the two of them in Elaine's home in June 1991, he
says that the family will heal more quickly if he is not there.
'When I'm there, the press will be there. We were never a close
family in the first place and, to satisfy the needs of the media
and the world, we suddenly had to become that.' He says that
sometimes he felt freer when he was locked up. 'Suddenly you
become possessed all over again to something that might not
have been there in the first place. Four and a half years of living
with no human warmth imprints on you deeply. You can't
suddenly turn around and be this person that they want you to
be. I've been a loner all my life and suddenly I've become a
brother, an uncle.'

For Brenda, her brother's release was like the birth of a baby. 'I feel Brian beginning to understand a lot of what we felt. We had to learn to talk again – that is a slow and painful process. I suppose in all the years you had a picture in you own mind about what Brian was going through. I've got to get on with my own life now and try and put all that to one side. You still want him there with you, but you have to think of the suffering that he is going through because of the others still in captivity.'

Elaine says that many people believed that their suffering was all over when he was released. 'People think that when all the hostages are home, Brian will be brilliant, but it also takes all the hostages to come home to help us. It's not over for us yet because we know what the other families are suffering. Ten months on and we're still struggling and suffering. The hostages are Brian's family.' They speak about the rebuilding of relation-ships: 'The only way that will completely happen is when all the hostages are released and settled within their own families.'

Brian Keenan talks about the bond of suffering which he shares with his sisters. He recalls telling his mother when he was in hospital that he needed to spend time on his own. 'There's a kind of quality of love which is indirect. As far as family readjustment and the healing of personalities goes, it's easier for everyone when we're not together. When we're together, it's still the hostage thing.'

They say that they still are not ready to go back to being a family. Brian says: 'Healing is easier when you are left to do it yourself. It's the terrible consequence of this situation that you fight for something for so long and then you have to let yourself go and stay away.' Brenda talks about how nice it would be to spend time together: 'All I want to talk about is ordinary everyday life as normal brothers and sisters do, and that's how it should be and sometimes I can't understand why it's not there.' She says that she is only now beginning to understand things Brian said at his press conferences in Dublin. 'At the time, it was a whole lot of big words. The one thing that I could understand was his words about John McCarthy. When John comes home, we will be suffering for his family.'*

The sisters talk about a party they had planned for Brian's homecoming. 'It couldn't happen because we felt so apart. If we had a party, it would have portrayed the wrong image because we would have to have been seen as three, but we are three individuals.' But Elaine does not want the family to revert back to being what it was before. 'Subconsciously you don't want to go back to that because in our family there was a lack of communication. If people cannot open up to each other, there is a problem. Our links with Brian were cut off for four and a half years and that has to be built. We are strangers in a lot of ways.' The sisters agree that, before Brian's abduction, they would have given little thought to the relationships within the family. 'It's coming to terms with the fact that there's a family there whether it's good or bad. Before, we knew that we would have to come together for some crisis or other. That's not a relationship. We would like that to change, as we have all changed.'

Brian talks about the freedom he finds when he drives his car, listening to all sorts of loud music: 'It's a constant sense of movement, of change, of which you are the controller and it can be done instantly. When you're driving, you can focus on the act itself and simultaneously apprehend the ongoing change

*John McCarthy was released on 8 August 1991.

148

around you. You can block out all the other antagonisms which you're forced to deal with.'

His sisters do not share in his pleasure. They spend most of their free time in the homes which have become shrines, in many ways, to the hostage issue. The television set, which showed hijackings, releases and moments of deep disappointment; the tattered press cuttings; the telephone, the lifeline which brought good and bad news; the endless stream of reporters calling into their homes. 'I would give a thousand pounds if I thought that I could get out in a car and do that,' said Elaine. 'We are coming back to the same four walls that haunted us. I still feel very strongly about it. You're still enclosed. It's too familiar and it can be bad news at times.'

This eight-hour conversation was also a time of revelation for Keenan. He believes that his sisters, particularly Brenda, went through a long period of hurt. Elaine, he admits, had her work as an outlet. 'The home has almost become a prison and that's the one that you don't break out of. Elaine had another way of ridding herself, but Brenda did not have that opportunity; she worried the life out of me. Everybody has got to find their own way at their own time . . . Attention is always well-meaning and Brenda had a harder time dealing with all of that.'

Brenda now feels that she is gradually returning to normal. She has thrown herself back into her woodwork classes which she abandoned for most of Brian's captivity. But she still has a problem switching off the television set at night. 'Mick has started turning it off, but he knows that I have to learn to do this myself.' The sisters agree that they and their families have changed, and Brenda talks about how things have changed with Mick: 'All my life, Mick was on a pedestal and I thought that everything that he said was right, but now I will argue back with him and it's not just over family problems but about world affairs. It's going to be very hard for Mick to accept that, but Mick has been out in the world and I haven't.' She wants to spend as much time as possible with her children to try to get to know them all over again.

Both women are glad to be out of the public eye, but there is still a long way to go. 'It gave me the chance to become a mother again,' Brenda said. 'You only realise afterwards that you had no life. You did not get time to think and talk to the children about the normal things in life.' Elaine Spence talks about the struggle to get back her own identity: 'I want to be seen for who I am and who I was before. So many people would say, "You are Brian Keenan's sister", and they did not know my name. I want back to the Elaine Spence that I was. Don't give me a label or a title because I have to lose that. It's slowly happening, but I think that you have to self-consciously decide that you want it to happen. Brian won't be here all my life and I have to go back to what I was before this all began.'

Brian Keenan talks about how he finds stardom repulsive: 'I just disappear, but Brenda and Elaine cannot do that, so they have to work even harder than me.' Elaine reckons that she is halfway there, but she believes that it will drag on for years: 'I don't think it will leave for the next several years anyway, but as long as people say, "You're Brian Keenan's sister, you're Elaine", I'm content with that.'

Yet the sisters see a positive side to their ordeal: 'I have experienced a lot of emotion in so many ways,' Brenda says. 'I feel sorry for people who haven't. A brother lost and found, the emotion in that alone.' She explains something she once gave to a reporter about how Brian built bridges and she and Elaine crossed over them. 'I just accepted that Brian was a community worker and I never accepted it when he used to talk about seeing the Catholic point of view. It was only when you started meeting ordinary women from the Catholic side that you realised that there is no difference. There may be as far as organisations are concerned, but not where the ordinary people are concerned. I am still talking to people about Brian and they say that all they want is the Troubles to be over. All they want is peace, a job and enough money to put food on the table, and peace of mind. If every person was honest, that would be all they would want – peace of mind, no more living in fear. For people who cannot put their hands out to others, this country is all wrong, all wrong.'

Before Brian was taken hostage, Brenda did not think much about such things. 'I used to live in a world of fantasy where everything was fine and I wanted everyone to be happy and to live together. I came out of myself and took steps that before I would never have taken.' She said that she learnt about the true extent of the bitterness and hatred in the North: 'I used to be proud of this country – that we used to have freedom of speech – but we no longer have that. You don't know who your enemy is. The squaddies think it's bad here not knowing who their enemy is, but the people don't know who it is. It is the person sitting next to you or listening to you.'

Elaine talks about two bridges she has built – an inner one and a political one: 'They're self-built bridges and there's no going back. I could not go back. It's now bred into my nature. If I go back over that bridge, I'm losing self-respect and that would be too much.'

One thing is certain. The four and a half years will never be replaced. 'You could spend a lot of time and a lot of money trying to make up for what we lost out on, but at the end of the day it might not work. We have to pick up what we have now.'